Beyond Tantra

Healing through Taoist Sacred Sex

Beyond Tantra

Healing through Taoist Sacred Sex

Mieke and Stephan Wik

FINDHORN
Press

First published by Findhorn Press in 2005

ISBN 1-84409-063-9

British Library Cataloguing-in-Publication Data.
A catalogue record for this book is available
from the British Library.

Edited by Kate Keogan
Cover design by Damian Keenan
Interior design by Thierry Bogliolo
Illustrations by Renild Ghys

Printed and bound by WS Bookwell, Finland

Published by
Findhorn Press
305a The Park, Findhorn
Forres IV36 3TE
Scotland, UK
tel 01309 690582/fax 690036
info@findhornpress.com
www.findhornpress.com

Contents

Disclaimer and Warning

In our experience, the exercises and techniques in this book can, if practised regularly, have a beneficial effect on your mental, emotional and physical health. However, the ideas, suggestions and techniques we describe are not intended as a substitute for medical advice; we do not provide diagnoses or suggest medication for any medical condition. If you have an existing medical condition, you should consult a physician before undertaking any of the physical exercises.

Please note that you may need to make changes in your life and relationship to allow Sexual Energy to flow and be a force for healing and development. In the process you will, most likely, be unable to avoid examining and dealing with some uncomfortable issues. This comes with the territory. Please proceed gently and with respect for yourself and your partner's ability to handle new information and skills. If at anytime you feel unsure or uncertain, simply slow down or stop. It may be the case that your mind and emotions need to catch up with your body or vice versa. On the other hand, it may be possible that you have stirred up something very deep and you may find that you're having difficulty dealing with an issue. In such a case you may want to consult a professional therapist.

Application of the concepts and exercises described in this book is at your, the reader's, sole discretion and risk.

About the Quotes from Lao Tzu

Lao Tzu (also spelled Lao Zi, Laozi or Lao Tsu) was a famous Chinese philosopher who is believed to have lived in approximately the 4th century BC. He is best known as the author of the Tao Te Ching. To the best of our knowledge, all the quotations from Lao Tzu in this book fall under the fair use or public domain guidelines of international copyright law.

An excellent resource for further research into the Tao Te Ching can be found at http://www.wayist.org/ttc%20compared/all_translations.htm

Please direct any queries concerning the quotes to info@beyondtantra.org

PART ONE

HEALING

Chapter 1

Tantra Workshop

The Tao's principle is spontaneity.
—Lao Tzu

The first time I ever heard the word 'Tantra' was in the early 1990s. One morning on my way to work I noticed a poster in the local bookshop advertising a Tantra course at the nearby course centre. I was intrigued. The poster indicated that the course was about 'a new way of working with sexual energy' but didn't say much more than that, except to state that no intimate contact would take place during the workshop.

Out of curiosity, I decided to enter the bookshop and have a look in the Sexuality section for any books they might have on Tantra. I'd never even noticed that section of the shop before so I was rather surprised to see quite a few titles there. I soon realized that this was a whole area of knowledge I knew absolutely nothing about. Three books caught my eye: two smaller volumes by a Thai author of Chinese descent, by the name of Mantak Chia, and a larger tome by a French woman called Margo Anand. I proceeded to buy the books and then I headed out to work.

I often ate lunch at the course centre's restaurant and so later that day at lunch time, over a bowl of soup, I asked my friends at the table if anyone knew anything about the course or was planning on going to it. A slightly embarrassed silence ensued and was finally broken by my friend John who said:

'You do know you need to be a couple to go on the course?'

'Oh, well, I guess that counts me out,' I replied. 'I can't imagine Mieke being up for such a course!'

Mieke and I had been married for over fifteen years at that point and I was pretty sure I knew what she would say if I asked her to go on a 'sex' workshop.

'So why not find someone else?' John asked.

I thought about this for a second. I then looked over at the table next to ours and saw an absolutely stunning young woman I had never seen before. She was obviously one of the centre's course guests. John, true to form, saw me looking at the woman and quickly understood that here was an excellent chance to tease me.

'Go on,' he said. 'Ask her.'

Well, I just didn't have the nerve to ask a woman to whom I had never spoken before to attend a 'sex' workshop with me. On the other hand, I was quite interested in going to the workshop. I decided that the only solution was to ask for a volunteer. I screwed up my courage, stood up, banged a spoon on my glass to get the room's attention and announced in a loud voice:

'I'd like to do the Tantra course this weekend. I need to find a woman to go to it with me since I understand that you have to be a couple to attend. Is there anyone here who might be interested in going with me?'

The room went very quiet. All of a sudden the young woman that I had been looking at stood up, looked at me, and said:

'I'd love to.'

John nearly choked on his soup!

I went over to the woman and introduced myself. Her name was Ruth and she was lively and outgoing. I immediately explained that this was a spur of the moment idea. I told her that I really did need to check with my partner first to make sure she was happy with the idea of my doing such a workshop with another woman even if, according to the poster, there was no intimate contact involved. That evening I told Mieke what had happened and asked her, with some nervousness, if it was OK for me to do the workshop together with the young woman. Much to my surprise she gave her blessing to the idea and told me to go and have fun. Mieke is an amazing woman!

The day of the course arrived and Ruth and I headed down to the ballroom of the large manor house in which it was being held. A German couple dressed in Indian clothing were running the course. After swearing us all to secrecy and confidentiality, they proceeded to set up a 'Tantric' atmosphere complete with incense, candles, cushions and Indian music. All the course participants were asked to wear colourful cloth wraps instead of our normal street clothes. For two days we learned about Tantric massage, the Yoni and the Vajra (Sanskrit names for the female and male sex organs respectively) and Shiva and Shakti (Indian deities). We danced and meditated. We did lots of gazing into each other's eyes.

At the end of it, I came away feeling a bit dazed. It seemed that in order to do this Tantra stuff I had to learn to become something I wasn't. I'm not Indian and I certainly didn't feel that I could suggest any of the things I had learned to Mieke. Somehow I just couldn't imagine us dressing up as Shakti and Shiva and dancing for each other. I also felt very uncomfortable with how the workshop was run. At one point the women were asked to dance bare-breasted in front of the men. There was one woman who refused to do this. The course leaders tried to convince her that it was OK and that it was an important part of the course for her to do this. The woman became more and more upset and was finally allowed to do the dance with her top on. I did not like watching this pressure being applied as I felt they were not respecting her. Much later I discovered that this woman had been sexually abused as a child and was just not able to show herself nude in front of a group of people.

So, my first taste of Tantra left me with a bit of a bad taste in my mouth. I did enjoy some of the exercises, such as learning how to breathe in the same rhythm as your partner, and the massage techniques. However, I was left with the feeling that, in order to 'do Tantra', I would have to dress up in Indian clothes and pretend to be someone that I'm not. This, together with what I felt was a lack of consideration towards the participants from the workshop leaders, meant that I pretty much gave up on the idea of Tantra.

I didn't throw the books out, however. When I got home, I had a quick glance through them. The Margo Anand book looked like it covered much the same territory as the workshop I had just attended. The Mantak Chia books didn't make much sense to me as they talked about Sexual Qi (the Taoist term for 'Sexual Life-Force Energy'), semen retention and other things which, at the time, I had no experience of and little interest in. I put them up on a shelf next to my other 'introduction to' type books where they gathered dust for the next eight years.

Oh, and what about lovely Ruth? I met her one last time a few months later in London. She told me she was off to Tunisia to live as the second (or was it the third?) wife of an Arab sheikh. She wasn't sure if it was such a good idea. I had absolutely nothing to say when she asked my advice (quite unlike me!).

Chapter 2

Healing Tao

To love someone deeply gives you strength,
Being loved by someone deeply gives you courage.
—Lao Tzu

Eight years later, my exploration of Sacred Sex started with re-reading those very same books I had bought before doing the Tantra workshop. This time it wasn't curiosity that drove me; it was an urgent need to know.

Mieke and I had moved to Ireland and were working hard at setting up a new business. We were under a large amount of stress, as the business needed a lot of attention. Mieke, who was forty-four at the time, became more and more tired and run-down. One day she told me that she wasn't feeling well at all. Her period had been unusually long and heavy and she was worried. I insisted that we go to see a doctor, much to her reluctance. Mieke has never liked going to doctors, and she took some convincing. But, in the end, she accepted that something was clearly not right and needed to be looked at.

When we arrived at the doctor's, Mieke described her symptoms. The doctor immediately referred her to a gynaecologist. We went to the gynaecologist the next day and, after a brief consultation, he announced that he wanted to perform an exploratory 'cleaning' operation on her. When I questioned this I was treated with something approaching contempt and told offhandedly that this was standard procedure. He then took a blood test to check Mieke's iron levels. When we phoned the following day, he told Mieke that the test showed that her iron levels were so low that she would have to take a course of iron supplements for three weeks before he could operate.

Mieke really didn't like what she was being told by the gynaecologist. She was adamant that she did not want to have an operation if there was any way that it could be avoided. She also had a feeling that she wasn't being given the whole picture. Over the twenty-plus years I had known her, I had learned that she would only say something about her inner feelings if she sensed something strongly. In this case it was very clear that she felt at a very deep level that the course of action suggested by the gynaecologist was not right for her.

Up until this time Mieke had always been very healthy and strong and never had any health problem like this. She had effortlessly borne four children and worked very hard and succeeded at being 'The World's Best Mum'. At the same time, she had always worked in quite stressful jobs and seemed to handle all of it with ease. So I was extremely worried and concerned about her. Something clearly had to be done and yet she did not want to go down the path being prescribed to her by Western medicine. I was in a quandary.

Now, as a person I've got a number of qualities and traits. Some of them are no doubt rather annoying at times, like my tendency to ask awkward questions. But one of my traits that can sometimes be quite useful is that, when I need to be, I can be very, very stubborn. I was not going to let the woman I loved suffer if I could do something about it. So I did the one thing I knew how to do: research. I read non-stop, for fourteen hours a day over the next two weeks, everything I could find on the Internet that had anything to do with menstrual problems, menopause, excessive bleeding, hormones or reproductive health. What I discovered, after reading a great deal on medical web sites, was that at least 75% of the women suffering from excessive menstrual bleeding should not, in the first instance, be operated on. According to what I read, excessive menstrual bleeding is most often not a mechanical problem, i.e. something physically wrong with the body, but rather has to do with the body's hormonal balance. If a woman's hormonal balance is disrupted, her menstrual cycle is often the first thing that starts to behave abnormally. Mieke also had many other symptoms, such as hot flushes, that indicated that she was indeed being affected by hormonal changes.

So I continued to read about the symptoms she was displaying and tried to discover whether they were a result of something physically wrong in the uterus that would warrant an operation. I soon found an article which suggested that an ultra-sound scan would be a wise thing to have done before having an operation, to see if there was any thickening of the uterine lining or if there were any growths in the womb. The article also suggested that, if one is not happy with a diagnosis one has received, it is a good idea to get a second opinion before deciding anything at all. As I continued to search, I also came across an intriguing site from a Dr. John Lee who advocated using something called 'natural progesterone'. According to him, this is a substance available from a wide variety of plant sources that, when extracted and applied as a skin cream, can be very helpful in restoring a natural hormonal balance. The cream is applied over a 28-day cycle and assists the body's hormonal release function. At this point I realized that I was in over my head. There were clearly options other than surgery but I had no idea which of them was the correct course to follow. I suggested to Mieke that we go back to the first doctor and tell her that we were not happy with what we had been told by the gynaecologist and that we should ask her if she could recommend anyone else. We did this the very next day. The doctor, somewhat to my surprise, was very sympathetic and referred us to a gynaecologist in the closest city, an hour's drive away. Luckily, we managed to get an appointment for the following week.

In the meantime, intrigued by what I had read about natural progesterone, I started to look into other natural, i.e. non-conventional, healing methods. It was then that I remembered that we already had a book about women and healing called *Healing Love through the Tao: Cultivating Female Sexual Energy* by Mantak Chia. It was one of three books I had bought before I did the Tantra course. I opened it up with new eyes. At this point I was no longer interested in the sex part of the book; now I wanted to know about healing. On the very first page he explains that the major way in which women lose energy is through menstruation. The book then provides detailed instructions on how to stop this loss of energy, using a combination of different exercises and techniques. I was amazed at what I was reading. At the same time, the sceptic in me instantly said, 'what if this is just a bunch of nonsense?'

So I decided to do yet more research. Was there any evidence available to show that this ancient Chinese (also known as Taoist) knowledge was anything more than old superstitions from a primitive culture? I spent yet more days reading everything I could about Traditional Chinese Medicine (TCM). This time I was overwhelmed by the quantity and quality of information that I found. I read that Acupuncture and Chinese Herbal Medicine had been used successfully not only by traditional healers, but had also been clinically tested and proven in Western universities. As far as I could tell, it appeared that Western medicine was also slowly but surely verifying that the Taoist view of the body and health (although not always making sense in accordance with the familiar, Western way) does indeed have an internal logic and consistency. A good deal of clinical evidence is now available to indicate that TCM cures work reliably in many cases. As a result, many health insurers in the West now cover acupuncture treatment.

The time arrived for our appointment with the second gynaecologist. He was obviously a busy man, as the waiting room was full of women, but luckily we were the first appointment of the day. We entered his office and explained to him why we were there and our concerns about the recommendation we had received from the first gynaecologist. I also told him what I had read about the possible hormonal causes of Mieke's condition as well as the recommendation that she should have a scan before going any further. He listened quietly and then said, much to my amazement:

'Firstly, I'd like to apologise for the state of the healthcare here in Ireland. We are woefully under-funded and, indeed, in some areas I feel like we are still providing a level of care that is of third-world quality. You're correct; there are other things that should be looked at first before operating and it is indeed quite likely that Mieke's condition has its origin in a hormonal disturbance.'

He went on:

'I'd like to arrange for an ultra-sound scan to ensure that there is nothing untoward in Mieke's uterus. I would like to prescribe a drug that she can take to help with her heavy bleeding, as she is clearly anaemic. I would also encourage her to take extra iron as the previous gynaecologist suggested. Also, I can see no harm at all in your trying the natural progesterone. I have a number of patients who have shown intolerance to the synthetic hormones we normally use in cases of hormonal imbalance and I'd be interested to know how you get on.'

We were completely amazed at his compassion, understanding and honesty. We felt like we, at last, had someone who was listening to us. I also felt that my research had been validated and this gave a real boost to my self-confidence and belief that I could help Mieke heal. With hindsight, I can clearly see that this doctor's willingness to be honest and straightforward with us was a real turning point and I am, to this day, very grateful to him. We left for home after thanking him very much.

Mieke went for an ultra-scan a few days later and we were relieved to hear the technician say, 'it looks fine to me' as he watched the display on the ultra-sound machine. On the way home, we bought some natural progesterone at the local chemist at the same time as collecting her prescription for the anti-bleeding drug. Mieke started a heavy period a few days later and we were delighted to discover that the drug which the gynaecologist had prescribed slowed her blood-flow dramatically. It looked like we had something to help with her worst symptom, at least.

During the following weeks, I continued to read the Mantak Chia book. Towards the end of the book there is a section on 'Traditional Lovemaking Positions and Healing'. This caught my attention and I read some of this aloud to Mieke. I asked her whether she thought that we should try some of the exercises from the book. She stopped what she was doing and looked straight at me as if I were totally crazy. With tears in her eyes she said:

'Here I am, with three-week-long heavy periods; I'm anaemic; on medication *and* I have absolutely no sexual energy at all and you want to do *what*?'

She paused for a few seconds and looked away. I felt rather foolish and regretted having said anything. What had I been thinking? Then suddenly, to my utter amazement, she looked up and said:

'OK – I think we should try it.'

I told you that she is an amazing woman!

So for the next six months we worked hard to follow not only the instructions in the Mantak Chia book but also some of the Tantra exercises in the Margo Anand book. At the same time, we followed the suggested rhythm for using the natural progesterone (three weeks on and one week off) and Mieke used the anti-bleeding drug when her flow got too heavy. She also started on extra iron and vitamin supplements. For many months it seemed like there was little or no improvement but at least Mieke's health wasn't getting any worse and the bleeding was under control.

One evening I was dutifully 'warming up the oven' (the Taoists have all sorts of expressions for different sexual activities, I soon discovered) by gently teasing Mieke's clitoris with my tongue. We had settled down into a routine of fifteen minutes' practice morning and evening and two longer, evening sessions –which could last up to four hours – every week. To be honest, not a lot was happening as result. Mieke was still having long, heavy periods and there was very little sexual energy happening between us. Still, we kept at it. Mieke is stubborn too!

That evening proved to be different, however. I was licking and teasing away as Mieke was lying on her back, listening to the gentle Nepalese music playing and visualising Sexual Energy flowing through her body. I was trying to concentrate and stay focused on the task at hand. All of a sudden, Mieke's entire body convulsed and I saw a bright flash of white light inside my head.

'What was *that*?' I asked, reeling slightly.

'I was just trying to get my Qi to connect in a loop as the book says I should,' she said. 'I think I just did it!'

Very soon afterwards, Mieke's periods started getting shorter and less heavy. Nine months later, she was back to normal and now, seven years later, she is completely healed and has more sexual energy and life-force then many women thirty years younger than her. She also looks ten years younger than her age. Our relationship has completely transformed for the better and I, too, am in much better physical and mental shape. To top it all off, the sex with Mieke is incredible!

Chapter 3

Ancient Traditions: New Understandings

The truth often sounds paradoxical.
—Lao Tzu

After so much research and reading, it was inevitable that we would start talking to our friends and family about what we had discovered. I soon found that I had to explain terms such as Sacred Sex, Taoism, Dual Cultivation, Tantra and Qi as these are not terms with which most people in the West are familiar. So before going into what I distilled from the large amount of (at times, conflicting) information I found during my research, I'd like go through some basic background definitions.

Sacred Sex

Sacred Sex is a fairly new term to describe practices that use sexual energy for healing and spiritual development. This energy can be created internally in one person as well as being generated between two (or more) people. Many cultures around the world have developed Sacred Sex practices, although few of them are well documented or, at least, any documents that may once have existed are no longer available. The Judaeo-Christian, Western civilization appears either to have completely lost or actively rooted out and suppressed any such tradition it may once have had.

The first question many people ask me when I talk to them about Sacred Sex is 'how does the connection between Sex and Spirit actually work?' This is totally understandable since so many people have been taught that Sex and Spirit are in opposition to each other. After all, it was not all that long ago that the Catholic Church taught that sex was sinful unless it was engaged in for procreation. My answer to this question is based on Mieke's and my practical experiences and is quite simple. I do accept, however, that before you have experienced it, it can sound a bit far-fetched. So bear with me, please, and suspend any disbelief for a second!

In my experience, spiritual development requires two things: intention and energy. You have to want to improve yourself otherwise it's just not going to happen. You also need to have the energy to do the work required, as it doesn't just happen by itself. The Sacred Sex masters of old discovered, probably through a process of trial and error together with keen observation, that sexual energy is the only type of energy that you can generate in your body without the addition of an external material substance. To generate all other types of energy you have to bring something from outside into your body such as food or air. Sexual energy has this remarkable quality of seeming to 'generate something from nothing'. Most people have experienced this feeling during and after orgasm. These masters observed that what actually happens is that, when you generate sexual energy, you connect directly to the huge reserves of energy around us in the Universe. I know; it does sound sort of strange that you could somehow plug-in to the energy that is 'out there'. But, in our experience, it does actually work. These masters then went on to discover that you can, indeed, use this sexual energy to support your intention to do spiritual work.

In other words, Sacred Sex does not mean that you can just engage in lots of sexual activity and automatically become healthier and more spiritually developed. In fact, just the opposite can be true. If you merely increase your sexual energy with the intention of 'having more fun', you may soon find that your health and state-of-being start to deteriorate as you will not be cultivating awareness of your use of sexual energy or filling up your energetic 'bank account'. Sacred Sex means what it says – using Sexual Energy in a sacred fashion. What this does require, for some people, is a redefinition of the term 'sacred'.

So does Sacred Sex mean that you have to 'believe' or 'have faith' in something? In my experience the answer is 'No'. What you do need, however, is a willingness to suspend your disbelief long enough to try some exercises and see for yourself whether they actually work. Remember that, if you had demonstrated a mobile phone to someone in the 15th century, you probably would have been burned at the stake as a witch or warlock, but mobile phones do actually work even if most of us do not have an in-depth knowledge of the physics involved.

The techniques of Sacred Sex have been used successfully for many millennia, so the chances are pretty good that there is some validity to them. But, at the end of the day, probably the best proof is that obtained by testing the techniques in the laboratory of your own relationship.

There are many Sacred Sex traditions – such as Chuluaqui Quodoushka (Shamanic American Indian) and Goddess worship practices (Isis in Egypt, Aphrodite in Greece) – but none of them have the same amount of literature and practitioners as Tantra and Taoist Dual Cultivation. In fact, if you browse the Tantra or Sexuality section in a bookshop that carries such books, you will soon discover that almost all of the available Sacred Sex literature falls into one of two traditions: Tantric and Taoist. This is partly due to the fact that these two traditions have the best historical documentation but also because these are the two traditions that have survived (just) into the present era.

Tantra

The Tantric tradition, often referred to as *Tantra*, originated in India but refers to practices used throughout South-East Asia. I found that it is quite difficult to pin down what Tantra actually is, since the term is used in many different ways. In this book I use the term 'Tantra' to refer to Indian sexual practices used for spiritual self-development.

In other words, Tantra is not just about better sex and bigger orgasms. Rather, it refers to a complete worldview in which the conscious use of sexual energy has an important role as a tool for spiritual development. What's interesting is that, when you start to explore the world of Tantra in the West, you soon discover that the vast majority of teachers and authors have some sort of connection to the teachings of an Indian self-styled guru called Osho, *a.k.a.* Bhagwan Shree Rajneesh (1931–1990). Osho was the founder and leader of a controversial new religious movement, who lived in India and the United States and published many books as well as founding a large commune in India.

One of the difficulties, then, with the term *Tantra* is that it is so often synonymous, in the West, with Osho's ideas about Tantra. This is not to say that Osho's ideas are all wrong; it's just that some of his teachings have little or no connection to classical *Tantra*. So the problem is that it is not that easy to get a clear picture of what the actual ancient teachings on Tantra contain just by reading an Osho-inspired book or going on a course given by Osho-followers. What confuses the picture even more is there are many different interpretations of Tantra even amongst traditionalists in India and Tibet. In this book, therefore, I will make a distinction between *Tantric* and *Neo-Tantric*. The first term refers to traditional Tantric wisdom as it was and is practised in India and Tibet, the second term to the flourishing community, often Osho-inspired, of Western teachers, workshop leaders and authors.

Taoism

Taoism (Daoism) is an ancient Chinese philosophy that has informed and guided Chinese culture for over five thousand years. *Tao* (pronounced 'dow' and also spelled 'Dao') means 'the way' or 'nature's way'. Taoism places emphasis upon spontaneity and teaches that everything in nature follows ways appropriate to itself. One of the fundamental tasks in life, according to this philosophy, is to discover our own way in harmony with nature or to 'become one with the Tao'.

> *A note about Chinese spelling: Before 1979, the most usual way to transliterate Chinese terms into English was based on the Wade-Giles system. 'Tao', 'Chi Kung' and 'Tai Chi' are all examples of Wade-Giles spellings. In 1979, the Pinyin system was adopted as the official system of Romanization in The People's Republic of China. 'Dao', 'Qi Gong' and 'Tai Ji' are all Pinyin spellings. However, many people still prefer to use the old spellings of 'Tao' and 'Tai Chi' while at the same time adopting the new spelling of 'Qi Gong'. In this book I have tried to use the most practical spellings while giving a preference to Pinyin unless the old spelling is widely used. For example, you probably won't find many 'Tai Ji' courses advertised but you will find 'Tai Chi'. There will be confusion in this area for many years, I suspect; I recently saw an ad for a 'tai ji /chi' course!*

Taoist philosophy is not the same thing as the Taoist religion, which developed later. In this book, the terms 'Taoist' and 'Taoism' refer to the philosophy, not the religion. Please note that this division between 'philosophical' and 'religious' Taoism is a fairly recent, Western concept. On a practical basis, all it means is that you should not expect to go to a Taoist Church and expect the priest there to be fully conversant with the subjects covered in this book, much as you would not expect a Catholic priest to know a great deal about the practices of the Cathars or Gnostics.

The early Taoists were keen observers of nature and humanity's place in it. They had a great interest in promoting health and vitality and put much emphasis on nurturing Qi (life-force). They developed many disciplines based on their findings. These disciplines are traditionally grouped into branches although not all traditions group in the same way. The following is a simplified list based on an amalgamation from various sources:

- Nei Dan (internal alchemy, meditation)
- Qi Gong and Tai Chi (moving meditation)
- Shuang Xiu (dual cultivation of sexual energy)
- I Ching (cosmology, astrology, divination)
- Yi Yua (acupuncture, Tui Na massage)
- Feng Shui (the use of environmental Qi)
- Fu Shi (Herbal medicine and Five Element Nutrition)
- The Arts (includes calligraphy, music and painting)

The first two branches are considered to be the oldest and most powerful and an aspiring Taoist would normally learn these first before moving on to any of the other practices. It would have been quite common for someone to study all eight branches in order to get a well-rounded education, as the narrow specialism we know in the West would not have been seen as desirable.

Taoism has had a far greater impact on Western civilization than many people realize. The I Ching (*The Book of Changes*) is one of the great classic texts of ancient China and is reputed to be 5,000 years old although no one is quite sure of its exact age. In 1697, Joachim Bouvet, a French Jesuit missionary who had been in China, introduced the I Ching to the German mathematician and philosopher, Gottfried Wilhelm von Leibniz. Leibniz was amazed by *The Book of Changes*. Its use of binary arithmetic (also known as Yin/Yang theory) was, at the time, unknown in Europe. This is how Western civilization was first introduced to binary arithmetic, which is not only the foundation of *The Book of Changes* but also the language of all modern computers. So the computer used to write and produce the book you are reading has been developed as a direct result of Taoist Yin/Yang theory. I find this fascinating.

Dual Cultivation (Shuang Xiu)

Dual Cultivation (Shuang Xiu) has been, until recently, a little known branch of Taoist knowledge. Dual Cultivation was traditionally considered part of the Inner Alchemy (Nei Dan) practices of self-cultivation. Taoist Inner Alchemy practices are used to promote spiritual development as well as physical health. This dual process of spiritual and physical development is also known as cultivating original nature and life. Dual Cultivation focuses on the conscious use, by a loving couple, of something known as Sexual Qi (sexual life-force) for health and spiritual development. Dual Cultivation appears to have reached its peak during the Han Dynasty (206 BC–220 AD), long before Buddhism had become widespread in China. In fact, some Taoist scholars are of the view that the practice of Dual Cultivation predates Taoism itself and was discovered during the very earliest days of Chinese civilization. However, the introduction of Buddhism (c. 67 AD), with its monastic and ascetic spiritual tradition, and the subsequent ascendancy (950–1050 AD) of Confucianism, with its rigid and moralistic ethos, put an end to the widespread practice of Taoist Dual Cultivation in China. It is only recently, in great part thanks to the works of Mantak Chia, Michael Winn and others, that these practices have again been brought to light.

> *For those readers with a more intimate knowledge of Taoist sexual practices, I'd like to make it clear that by Dual Cultivation (shuang xiu) or, specifically, paired man and wife cultivation (fu fu shuang xiu), I am referring to the inner alchemy practice of using sexual energy for healing and spiritual development. I am not using the term Dual Cultivation to refer to other, later, Chinese practices such as the bedchamber arts (fang zhong) and the somewhat more controversial practice of gathering (cai pu) of Sexual Qi from unknowing partners.*

Qi and TCM

Qi (also spelled 'Chi') is a fundamental, East Asian concept. A direct translation of Qi from the Chinese would be 'air' or 'breath', but Qi is also used to mean the life-force or 'spiritual energy' that is part of everything that exists. Qi is also known as *Ki* in Japanese and *Prana* in Sanskrit. There is no accepted proof of the existence of Qi in the Western world as, in this culture, the concept simply does not exist. There is also no direct translation for Qi in English. The Taoists weren't actually all that concerned with analysing and defining Qi. Instead, they invested the bulk of their effort in observing its flow and learning how to work with it. The Taoists observed that, with a good reserve of Qi, you can remain healthy and live a long life. Working with Qi is at the heart of all of the Taoist disciplines, such as Acupuncture, Feng Shui, Martial Arts and Dual Cultivation. Sexual Qi is simply a particularly powerful form of Qi generated in the human body.

During my research, I found that it was much easier to get a coherent understanding of the theory behind Taoist Dual Cultivation than it was of the theory behind Tantra. This is because, as mentioned above, Tantra developed from a religious background and, as with many religions, there are many different and, at times, conflicting descriptions of the practices. In contrast, Dual Cultivation and Traditional Chinese Medicine (TCM) are based on a common understanding of the human body and its energy systems. This means that it is much easier to crosscheck and verify its internal consistency. All of the fundamental concepts – such as Qi, the Meridians, the Tan Tien and the Small Orbit – are identical whether you approach the subject from Acupuncture, Qi Gong, Martial Arts, Dual Cultivation or any of the Taoist branches of knowledge.

The Difference between Tantra and Dual Cultivation

Tantric and Dual Cultivation methods and techniques have many similarities once you remove their religious and cultural wrappings. There is one major difference, however. Tantra is primarily a method for raising Sexual Qi up the spine to create a state of ecstasy. For many people this can be a religious or spiritual experience as well as an incredibly powerful way of working with Sexual Qi. Dual Cultivation also works with moving Sexual Qi up the spine; the fundamental difference between the Tantric and the Taoist methods is that the Taoist techniques move the Sexual Qi back down the front of the body to complete the 'Xiao Zhou Tian'. This circular movement of energy has been translated as 'Microcosmic Orbit', 'Small Heavenly Circulation' or 'Small Orbit'. This circulation of Qi has a profound healing and energizing effect as the generated energy is packed or stored back into the body.

Tantra therefore focuses on the ecstatic release of sexual energy and is quasi-religious, sometimes at the expense of the physical body. Dual Cultivation, on the other hand, is a method of using sexual energy to promote good health and longevity as well as spiritual development. This is an important point that is very often not made clear, especially when reading Tantric source material and later Neo-Tantric books and other instructional material.

A Western Scientific Explanation for Sacred Sex

After all this research into Eastern philosophies, I was still left with the question of 'How do the techniques of Sacred Sex actually work?' I had studied the Taoist and Tantric texts at length and verified through solo and dual practice that the techniques function when practised diligently and as described. So it was clear that Eastern adepts had identified and accurately documented ways of managing Sexual Qi. But what is actually going on in our body when we use these techniques? I then found some research that sheds a great deal of light on the subject; John C. Lilly M.D. (1915–2001), one of the world's foremost brain researchers, carried out some groundbreaking research involving the pre-optic nucleus portion in the brain that contains the sexual system. In males, this controls erection, orgasm, and ejaculation – each in a separate place – while farther back, in the mesencephalon, the three are integrated and fired off in sequence. He demonstrated that the orgasm and ejaculation could be triggered separately by stimulating these different brain areas.

So it appears that the Taoists and Tantrikas discovered, through a process of experimentation over hundreds of years, that it is possible to guide our internal electrical energy to different sections of our brain, just as Lilly proved with electrodes. There will be a lot of practical information later in the book about how to do this (without electrodes!). What about the female brain? There is a lot of evidence that points to clear differences in the structure of male and female brains. Most of this seems to indicate that women do not have the same 'compartmentalization' in their brains as men. The female brain is less concentrated and utilizes significant portions of both hemispheres when it is engaged in a task. This would explain why 'relationship' is so important to women! Later in the book I'll show how to use this understanding in a practical way when learning how to generate Sexual Qi.

So how does this flow of Sexual Qi work? Well, thoughts are basically electrical signals. This means that each thought generates a very small amount of current. This current has an effect on the tissue of your brain. I saw an amazing picture recently of brain scans done on meditating Tibetan monks. These images show very clearly that meditating has a powerful, measurable effect on the brain. It's not a great leap to imagine that if, instead of meditating, you direct your awareness elsewhere, such as visualizing a circuit through your body, you actually create a circuit. It may be quite a weak circuit to start with but what happens is that over time, and with practice, it gets stronger and stronger. If this circuit then stimulates areas of the brain that are connected to sexual and 'spiritual' pleasure, then you will experience exactly what the Taoists and Tantrikas describe.

It appears, therefore, that there is not only a large body of Eastern knowledge but also Western scientific research to confirm that the conscious direction of internal electrical energy can, and does, have a beneficial effect on our bio-electrical systems. My personal conclusion from my research is that I'd rather practice Sacred Sex than have an electrode inserted into my pre-optic nucleus! I did find it reassuring, however, to find that there is Western research to indicate that there is a scientific basis to Sacred Sex.

Putting It All Together

At the end of the day, I found that the Tantric tradition is very interesting for what it teaches about using Sexual Qi for ecstatic sexual experiences and spiritual development, but it doesn't have a whole lot to say about health or grounding sexual energy on a day-to-day basis. The Taoist tradition, on the other hand, has a great deal to say about health and energy-grounding and therefore ended up as the cornerstone of our Sacred Sex work. However, the Neo-Tantrics do fill in an important gap. Many of the modern Tantra courses use skills and exercises from the Human Potential Movement that are very useful when learning how to deal with (and heal) some of the emotional and communication issues that inevitably arise when working with sex and relationship. Finally, Western healing science (both conventional and alternative) is making great strides in understanding how our bio-chemical systems work. This book is a practical synthesis from all four of the above traditions.

Why this book?

After Mieke healed, I soon found that our friends started to ask us about her recovery and how she had done it. They also wanted to know how we managed to keep our relationship together after so many years and after so many challenges and why we seemed to be so full of sexual energy. I soon noticed that their eyes would often start to glaze over as I launched into a complete rundown of Dual Cultivation and Taoist Sexual Energy Practices. All that detail about meridians, Qi, acupuncture points, breathing and Yin/Yang theory was a bit much for a short conversation! I discovered that people understood much better if I just explained the core concepts that we had distilled and used.

One day I found myself explaining what we had discovered to yet another person. She stopped me and said, 'That's amazing; you two really should write a book about what you've done and discovered.' I thought about that for a while and then thought, 'OK – why not? If we can share what we've learned with other couples, that would be nice!'

So here it is. What Mieke and I have attempted to do is document, as clearly as we can, what the two of us have learned from our many years of exploration of Sacred Sex, and Taoist Dual Cultivation in particular. We have made no attempt to beat around the bush or avoid the difficult bits. The simple truth is that if you start working with the techniques of Sacred Sex, you will most likely have to make some pretty fundamental changes to yourself and your relationship. Mieke and I have never met anyone who has not had this experience. The good news is that it can be done gently and at your own pace. Yes, there is stretching involved and, as with all stretching, it can be a bit painful at times. Our experience, which I hope you will have as well, is that the payback is well worth the investment. I hope you have as much fun with the journey of exploration as we have had. It's not necessarily always easy and without challenges but we certainly found that it was worth the effort.

A Word on Authority

One of the most frustrating things I discovered when researching Sacred Sex, Taoist Dual Cultivation and Tantra, is that it is difficult to locate authoritative information. Sacred Sex is not a recognized science in the West and there are no peer-reviewed journals to fall back on. There are literally hundreds of books and even instructional videos on the market from self-styled experts but it's not easy to know what is valid, authentic information. As I have already mentioned, there is a great deal of material available concerning Traditional Chinese Medicine, but there is not much information about Dual Cultivation in those books. There are odd allusions here and there to 'controversial sexual techniques of dual cultivation' but that's about it.

When I have spoken directly to both Western and Chinese internal energy practitioners from the Taoist lineage, I have been met with either ignorance or reticence when it comes to awareness of this area of Taoist energy work. In particular, the Chinese I have spoken to often acknowledge its existence but say things like 'we leave this area to couples as it quite a private matter in China'. They then tend to change the subject hastily. So, despite our best efforts, we have not been able to locate any living Chinese teachers of Dual Cultivation. This does not mean that they don't exist; it's just that, if they do, they're not easy to find. Maybe if I spoke Chinese it would help but I'm not so sure! We have also had both good and not-so-good experiences with Western teachers of Tantra and Dual Cultivation. We have consistently heard and read tales of mixed results from other people as well. It does seem that good Sacred Sex teachers are hard to find.

I would therefore like to make it very clear to our readers that Mieke and I do not claim to be Masters of Taoist Dual Cultivation. In fact, I was seriously considering writing a chapter called 'How to act like a complete twit with no brain when it comes to sex' to document some of the disasters I've had over the years! Any authority we have comes simply from the fact that we have used the techniques for many years and found, to our own satisfaction, that they work as described. I can also confirm that the energy-work system used is in great accordance with what I have learned through studying Acupuncture, Qi Gong, Tai Chi and Chinese Herbal medicine. We're sharing what we have discovered in a spirit of humbleness and gratitude to the many thousands of men and women who have spent so much time over the centuries exploring and documenting the techniques of Sacred Sex. We are, literally, in their debt.

PART TWO

PRACTICE

Chapter 4

Getting Started

The exercises in this book, although presented sequentially, actually cover many skills at the same time. For example, creating trust, removing energetic blocks and increasing sensitivity are just some of the things you will practise in each exercise. Learning Sacred Sex is like learning a musical instrument, i.e. you learn the basics, you practise regularly and you add new skills as you go along. It can feel, just as with learning an instrument, as if not much progress is being made at times. This is normal, as it is often difficult to gauge your own progress. So expect that there will be times that you'll need to be persistent and persevere. Dual Cultivation is not a quick fix, but the results are well worth any resistance you may need to overcome. Have patience with yourself, and be thankful you don't have to spend nine years in a cave like some of the old Taoist and Tibetan monks and nuns!

There is one other important similarity to learning to play an instrument. If you get stuck, don't push. As a musician, I have often found that when I come to a difficult musical passage, it is only useful to push myself to a certain point. If I push too hard I run the risk of learning how to play the notes incorrectly, which makes it even harder to get it right later. It works much better to wait and try again the next day as, nine times out of ten, it is much easier to approach something fresh the next time. The same applies to the exercises in this book. Give them a try, and if you feel stuck, just stop what you're doing and try again later. There's no 'should' or 'must' involved. It's all about learning to 'go with the flow' as the Taoists would say.

About the PRACTICE Chapters

Each **practice** chapter is divided into sections. I suggest that both partners read through all the chapters before they start the practical work. If you're the kind of people who like to discuss things with each other, then go ahead and talk about what you've read and what you think and feel about it. The more you can open the lines of communication, the better.

The Understanding

The *Understanding* presents a fundamental concept of Dual Cultivation.

The Background

The *Background* gives examples, historical references and analogies to clarify the concept presented in the *Understanding*.

Our Stories

In this section, Mieke and I will tell you a story or two from our own journeys towards the understanding presented in each chapter.

The Exercise

These are hands-on, detailed descriptions of the techniques and practices we use in Dual Cultivation practice. In many of the exercises, I've included some sample dialogues in a separate box. You may find these useful if you find yourself 'stuck for words' but these dialogues are not intended as 'this is how you do it' templates. Hopefully, you can use them instead as food for your own creative process if required.

Solo Cultivation and Same-Sex Dual Cultivation

This book is about Dual Cultivation, *i.e.* the cultivation of Sexual Qi between two people. Although this most often refers to a man and a woman, the

Taoist texts do have references to same-sex cultivation. The techniques of Dual Cultivation can be used just as well by Gay and Lesbian couples and this book should hopefully be of use to them, although some exercises will not be applicable.

For those readers without partners or whose partners may not be inspired to join you (yet) in Dual Cultivation practices, there is the option of Solo Cultivation. In this case you practise self-stimulation rather than working with a partner to generate Sexual Qi. In fact, Solo Cultivation is often recommended in the Taoist texts, even for people in a sexual relationship, as a way to learn to work more consciously with your own Sexual Qi.

A Note on Terminology

I've tried to keep this book simple and straightforward and have used English terms and phrases as much as possible. There are some terms that are not translatable from other languages and I'll explain them as they occur. I've also tried to be consistent in the spelling of Chinese terms that have different spellings in use. For example, I use 'Qi' instead of 'Chi'.

Another issue around terminology is the unfortunate fact that most of the words used for the human sexual organs in English are either clinical or have a negative connotation. Sadly, this is a pretty accurate reflection of Western society's attitudes to human bodies and sexuality. In this book, I use the Sanskrit term 'Yoni' for the female sexual organ, i.e. the vagina, and the Taoist term 'Jade Stalk' for the penis. Feel free to use any terms you like as long they have a good feeling about them both for you and your partner.

Chapter 5

Dealing with Belief Demons

The Understanding

> Those who know others are intelligent,
> those who know themselves are truly wise.
> —Lao Tzu

Almost all people in modern Western cultures have negative thoughts, beliefs, conditioning and 'body knowledge' about sex and sexuality. These beliefs are deeply stored both in our minds and our bodies. In order to practise Dual Cultivation successfully, we need to be prepared to exchange these negative beliefs for positive ones.

This is easier said than done, as many of our core beliefs are deeply held. A good place to start this process is to identify our current beliefs about sex and see if we are open to letting new, positive beliefs replace any outdated, negative or no longer helpful ones.

The Background

The teachings that form the core of Dual Cultivation are based on the view that Sexual Qi is fundamentally a neutral force that can be used in many ways. Just like electricity can be used to light a house or to shock someone, it's all about using it wisely. Many cultures discovered thousands of years ago that Sexual Qi can be used to promote physical, emotional and spiritual development. Unfortunately, this knowledge was later actively suppressed by many organized religions and other sex-negative organisations and replaced with the notion that 'Sex is Evil'. For the majority of people in the developed world today, sexuality is, at best, confusing and, at worst, a source of self-loathing and conflict. So we've ended up becoming our own worst enemies when it comes to trying to deal in a positive, open manner with our sexuality. The demons are well and truly inside us.

The reality is that most people have a pretty confused set of images and beliefs when it comes to their sexuality. This confusion has often been created during their childhood and is constantly reinforced by the media. It's no wonder, then, that many people go to a weekend Tantra course, have a wonderful time, come home and then discover that it all just fizzles out. It's just not that simple to replace the negative with the positive. Just lighting a few candles and practising some new sexual positions is not going to make much of a difference if you have core beliefs such as 'sex is dirty' or 'good girls/boys don't like sex' or 'sex is not spiritual'. As so many spiritual teachings say: 'Before the new can make its presence felt you need to get rid of the old.' In the case of Sacred Sex, this means that a good first step is to take a long, judgement-free look at yourself and understand, compassionately, where you are starting from. Once you've had a good look at your demons, you've got a much better chance of dealing with them.

Mieke's Story

'I'm responsible for my own sexuality.' I've heard this phrase many times now. Before Stephan and I started working with Sacred Sex, I had not thought much about it really, especially not in relation to myself. In my mind, sex was something you did with your life partner. To have sex with someone, you would need to be in love, or at least have strong loving feelings for each other. One of the things I clearly remember my mother telling me was how important it was for a woman to keep the man happy. She did not say it out loud, but I knew she meant especially in bed. I also heard her say that it was not important how the woman felt, what she wanted, or did not want. The man's happiness and satisfaction were what mattered. I also acquired a lot of unspoken beliefs from family, friends, and society.

At the time when Stephan and I started working with Dual Cultivation, I thought that I was, when it came to sexual matters, quite progressive in my thinking. What I soon discovered was that what I thought did not really match up with what I was feeling. I discovered that I am one of those people who learns best by doing something, through body experience. Yet here I was, practising and learning new communication skills and new Sacred Sex techniques, and really struggling with them. I was shy, I felt useless, I often felt unwilling to go along with things. I heard a part of me telling myself, 'A good girl does not do that!'. I became more and more aware of these old beliefs from my childhood and began to identify quite a long list of why I should not enjoy an orgasm and why I should never reveal my pleasure to my partner.

I decided that I wanted to do something about this. I found that just sharing it with Stephan was not going to help me get rid of these old beliefs that definitely did not serve me anymore. One day, during one of his many research sessions on the Internet, Stephan found an interesting course for women like me. The course was designed for mature women who want to heal the separation between the sacred and the sexual. He encouraged me to go, and I'm happy to say I agreed.

Over the next six months, I participated in three workshops with around twenty-five other women, all from very different backgrounds and countries, mostly around my age, i.e. forty-five to fifty-five. We danced, meditated, laughed and cried together. We went for walks in nature, spent time in solitude and quiet, shared thoughts and experiences. In a safe and controlled environment, we also participated in exercises where we shared sexual pleasure and orgasm with each other.

The course leader, a woman, was very skilled at gently pushing us beyond our limits. If we asked the question 'why?' about anything, she would answer: 'why not?' Under her guidance, we used sexual energy to blast through old patterns and thought-forms that we no longer wanted or found useful to us. I found that I was not the only one who was hanging on to all these old patterns and beliefs; the other women felt just as I did. And we all wanted to move forward into freedom, sexual freedom, away from all the old conditioning around men, around our partners.

In this very safe and supportive environment we helped and encouraged each other to dare do something new, however scary it felt. For me it was a great gift to be able to spend this time away from my everyday life, and discover what it was like to be with a group of women. I was amazed by the openness and total honesty between us. I learned so many things. I pushed my boundaries, and by doing so became much more in touch with who I really am. One of the most important things I learned was that I am indeed responsible for my own sexuality. How can I interact and communicate honestly with my partner if I'm not clear with myself, if I don't understand my own sexuality and know what I like and want?

On my return home, I was able to bring my new insights and experiences back to our relationship. I felt lighter and more in touch with my body. I felt that I had taken another step in creating a more harmonious and joyful relationship.

Stephan's Story

Mieke and I come from very different backgrounds. She was raised in a very traditional Roman Catholic family whereas I grew up in a liberal, freethinking environment. I was nineteen and she was twenty-three when we met and fell in love (yes, it was 'love at first sight'). Up until the point Mieke fell ill, I had never really spent much time trying to understand what culture she had come from or how that had affected her. At times, of course, I had been completely baffled by her responses and ways of doing things but I had always put this down to the inevitable difficulties I assumed any cross-cultural relationship must have.

When we started to work with the Sacred Sex teachings, I soon discovered that we had radically different viewpoints in a number of areas. Even though we had always tried very hard to be progressive and enlightened, it turned out that a great number of negative thoughts about sexuality were still very much alive and kicking in both of us. A typical example was my negative belief, learned in childhood, that 'women don't really like sex; they just do it to keep men happy'. This meant that, when I finally did find a woman who consented to have sex with me, I worked as hard as I could to try and make her happy, since I believed that 'she doesn't really want to do this but, if I get her excited enough, maybe she will enjoy it after all'.

When Mieke and I started to talk about our beliefs I discovered, much to my surprise, that she really did like sex. I also found out that she was quite frustrated that I was so goal-oriented and couldn't just relax enough to give her time to warm up a bit since I was so worried about getting her excited. Once I finally heard and understood this, we both realized that we did have some common understanding to work with. So a bit of communication made a huge difference when we finally got around to it!

The Belief Awareness Exercise

Goals

- Develop a greater self-awareness of your core sexual beliefs.
- Learn more about your partner's beliefs.

Duration

About 30 minutes

Description

This exercise is described as a two-person activity, but you can do it by yourself if you like. Both partners take two blank sheets of paper and a pen. Put the second sheet to one side for the moment.

On the first sheet, write a list of statements that reflect what you have been taught or have learned about sex as a child up to the age of puberty. What you're interested in is information that was given to you by others, not discoveries of your own. Here are some questions you can start with:

- What did my parent(s) tell me about my body and sex?
- What did I learn in school about sex?
- What did my friends tell me about sex? (or what did I guess they were saying?)
- What things did I learn about men and sex?
- What things did I learn about women and sex?

and, most importantly,

- What did I learn about sex that no one ever actually said to me in so many words?

Go ahead and list as many points as you like.

When you are done, go back through the list and ask yourself whether you intellectually still agree with each belief. Then ask yourself if your body agrees with the belief.

What does 'body agrees with the belief' mean? It's quite simple really. When Mieke and I started working with the Dual Cultivation practices, it often happened that I would read about something, discuss it, try it and then find out that it didn't work. This was a great puzzle, and a bit discouraging since I was sure I had understood the instructions. After a while I realized that, just because I understood something with my mind, it didn't mean that my body understood it or necessarily 'agreed'. As someone with a strong intellect, this had always been a bit of a frustration but, until I started working with Dual Cultivation, I had usually managed to succeed at most anything through sheer mental willpower. I soon discovered, of course, that you can't do that when working with Sexual Qi. You can't will an erection, and you certainly can't force an orgasm.

Instead, you need to learn a delicate, graceful dance that involves creating the right conditions for your body to unlearn, and relearn. It means becoming much more aware and sensitive to what your body is telling you at any given moment and accepting that your 'being' is much greater than just your mind. For many people this is completely obvious; for others it is a bit of a revelation. It certainly can be a revelation when you discover that your body has a mind or belief system of its own.

How do you check a body belief? One way is to remember a situation where a belief was brought into play and recall what your actual response was. For instance, you may have a belief that 'sex is good, clean fun'. If you notice that every time you make love you instantly get up and rush to the shower, then this could be a good indication that some part of you thinks that you have engaged in an unclean activity. The trick then is to observe telltale signs of inconsistency between your beliefs and your actions without judging yourself. You might want to try to have compassion with yourself as you do this as everyone, at one time or another, has internal struggles between their mind and body. Sex just happens to be one of the major areas where these struggles get played out.

Another practical example of the difference between mind and body belief is one that emerged when Mieke did the exercise. In her list she wrote a statement:

'Good girls don't wear sexy, revealing clothing.'

When she looked at this to see if she agreed or disagreed with it now, she discovered that with her mind she didn't agree with the statement at all. Lots of perfectly nice, good women wear sexy clothes and she has never had a problem with this. When she examined her body belief she realized that sometimes when she wears sexy clothes part of her is still uncomfortable and there are traces of the old shame that was handed to in her childhood.

Now, bring yourself back to the present. With your list in front of you:

Put a '1' next to each belief with which both your mind and body still agree.

Put a '2' next to each belief with which your mind disagrees but your body still agrees.

Put a '3' next to each belief with which your mind still agrees but your body disagrees.

Put a '4' next to each belief with which your mind and body both disagree.

When you are finished, take the second sheet of paper. Draw a vertical line to create two columns and label the left-hand column 'Coherent' and the right-hand column 'Incoherent'.

Now copy all of the statements that you have put a '1' or a '4' next to into the 'Coherent' column and all the statements that you have put a '2' or a '3' next to into the 'Incoherent' column.

When you are finished scoring and copying, take turns reading your lists to each other. First read to each other your coherent beliefs and then read your incoherent beliefs. Try to avoid making any comments or discussing anything that you hear. Simply listen to the information you are being given.

When you are done, go back and have a look at your incoherent beliefs. Which ones can you identify as no longer useful or downright unhelpful to developing a positive view of sexuality? Can you write down some new beliefs with which you might replace them?

The point of the exercise is not to change all of your beliefs suddenly. It's simply about opening up your mind to the possibility that you may need some new beliefs or understandings about sex. When you are done, file the lists away in a safe place. It can be interesting to go back and have a look at them when you have finished all the exercises in this book and see what, if anything, has changed.

Chapter 6

Building Trust

The Understanding

> He who does not trust enough,
> will not be trusted.
> —Lao Tzu

Strong sexual feelings and powerful emotions are intimately connected. If you experience fear or anxiety when your Sexual Qi flows, you will tend to revert to actions that allow you to feel safe. These actions are often based on old habits or, if you are under severe threat, instinctive reactions based on your primitive fight or flight mechanism.

These old habits or instinctive reactions are often not useful if you wish to practice Sacred Sex as they do not allow you to make clear, conscious and informed choices. One way to reduce fear and anxiety is to have a trust-filled relationship. This creates a safe space for Sexual Qi to flow. An excellent way to build informed trust is to practise clear and accurate communication.

The Background

For most people, it's not that easy to have trust in your own ability to handle sexual energy. Many people can identify experiences, often from childhood, where their normal curiosity about sex and sexuality landed them in situations where they were 'in over their heads' in one way or another. A quite normal reaction to these experiences is to pull back or retreat and to exhibit much greater caution the next time a sexual encounter happens. When this happens over and over again, we build up very deep patterns and habits that are hard to break even with the best will in the world. These patterns and habits are useful for protecting ourselves but not so useful when we want to start learning how to generate and channel Sexual Qi.

It is possible to unlearn these habits and patterns but it takes courage and determination. You also need to have a situation that provides physical, emotional, mental and sexual safety. If you don't feel safe, it's just not possible to open up to areas of yourself that are very vulnerable. We discovered that it was impossible to start on the path of Sacred Sex until we had found a way to create a safe, trusting space where we could be open and honest with each other. The exercise in this chapter helps to build that trust on an intellectual and emotional level. The exercises in the next chapter help build trust on the physical level.

Stephan's Story

When Mieke became ill and I started to research Sacred Sex, I took out the three books on Sacred Sex that I had bought some years earlier. I started by reading through them fairly quickly until I came to the interesting bits where the actual sex exercises were. I figured we were liberal and progressive enough not to need to do all of those communication and trust-building exercises. Well, after a few months not much was happening. It felt like we were going through the motions but none of the things that were supposed to happen according to the books were happening. No female orgasms, no increased sense of well-being, nothing at all. Mieke was frustrated and I was frustrated.

So I went back to the books and read again, a bit more slowly this time. While I was reading, I tried to observe myself as if from a distance. I watched myself to see what sections of the book I was skimming over and, when I caught myself doing this, I stopped. I then went back and re-read the section in question, word for word. After doing this a few times I discovered that the parts I was avoiding were all the things that had to do with looking at myself and my own patterns, my beliefs around sexuality and, most importantly, learning how to communicate with my partner. I was so concerned with learning how to do something new that I was completely missing the bits that had to do with sorting out the old.

And so, very hesitantly, I broached the subject with Mieke during a long car ride back from Dublin to the west coast of Ireland. The roads are pretty bad in some parts of Ireland so that a journey that would take two hours anywhere else in Europe can take four or more hours. Plenty of time for a long chat!

I said: 'You know, one of the exercises I was reading in the book has nothing to do with physical sex. Instead it encourages you to tell each other about past sexual experiences that you really enjoyed as a way of getting to know more about what each of you really like.'

Mieke went very quiet. After a few minutes she said, 'I don't think that's such a good idea.'

'Why not?' I asked.

'If I do, I'm afraid you'll get very angry,' she said.

My heart sank. In an instant I realized that we had a huge problem that we would have to deal with if we were going to get working on our sexual relationship. Ten years previously, Mieke had started, without my knowledge, a sexual relationship with another man that had lasted for five years. When I finally found out about it, I was very upset and angry and we had separated for six months as a result. After some counselling, we decided to try and start again which we had done reasonably successfully. But at that instant I realized that the wounds were not all healed and were in fact still very much present. I had a strong sense as well that this unresolved issue was at the very heart of why we were still struggling on many levels of our relationship. To put it simply, I still didn't trust her and she was still afraid of my verbal and emotional anger. I understood that this was not a good place from which to start working with Sacred Sex and, if we wanted to proceed, something had to be done about it.

'What could I do to make it safe for you to tell me?' I asked.

She responded, 'Well, you would need to promise me that, if I tell you about my experience, you will never, ever bring it up again or talk about it. I don't want it to be used against me.'

When I heard this, I saw that she was afraid, as she had every right to be, that I would use something like this as ammunition in a future argument. I saw that I had often done this in the past and that my behaviour made it very difficult for her to trust me and show any vulnerability. It wasn't a pretty picture of myself that was being painted. I then asked myself if I could make such a promise. I wasn't really sure but I wanted to believe that I could and said as much.

Much to her credit she trusted me to keep my promise and proceeded to tell me a pretty nice story about an experience she had had with her lover. I learned something about her that I didn't know and I've kept my promise. Within days our exercises started to show results. Much to my amazement, she had an orgasm, the first with me for many years. That experience showed us, in a pretty dramatic fashion, that if you are willing to trust you can free up sexual energy.

Mieke's Story

It's a clear, starlit night. Stephan and I are driving along the windy road from Dublin back to our home on the west coast of Ireland. It feels cosy and mesmerizing to follow the curves in the road and the contours of the hills on either side. There is not much oncoming traffic and the road is quiet. It feels safe just to sit in the car listening to the engine purring. On long drives we often drive in silence while listening to music. At other times, we have long conversations. This was one of those 'long conversation' drives.

We've just started a new stage in our lives and have decided to work with some sexual energy exercises to help me heal a health problem I'm having. This was not an easy decision as I have very little energy, let alone sexual energy! We've lived together for many years travelling, having children and working. During all that time there has been one subject that I feel was taboo for us to talk about: the love affair I had with another man in the past. I had never been able to talk about what it had been like for me, what it had meant to me and how it did not in any way diminish my love for Stephan.

So when Stephan suggests, as we're driving along, that we do a communication exercise from one of the books called 'tell your partner about a peak sexual experience', I find myself going quiet. This is too difficult for me! I just can't do it!

I sit in silence as thoughts race through my head: Do I have to tell him about an experience with him? Or dare I tell him about an experience with another man?

I very much want to break this taboo between us. But I'm worried. I want to know that, if I do tell him about a peak sexual experience, what I say will not be used against me at a later time. I can still remember what Stephan said angrily when he finally knew about my relationship: 'I always knew you had sexual energy with other men but not with me!'

I share my fears with Stephan and he reassures me: 'This is an exercise in building trust. I will just listen to you and I won't judge; I won't react and I won't criticize.' I decide to trust Stephan. I take a deep breath to rid myself of the knots in my stomach. I am nervous because somewhere deep down I know that this is an important moment in our relationship.

I hesitate and then begin to tell him about a peak sexual experience I had with another man. I tell him what was important and pleasant for me, what aroused me and what made me happy. I have never been able to do this before and it is a totally new experience for me to be able to speak so openly with him. I feel a huge relief at being able to talk about this. When my story is finished, there is a long silence. I feel acceptance from him.

Something important has happened. It is the first but not the last of many more intimate and deep conversations to come.

The Accurate Listening Exercise

Goals

- Build trust in your relationship
- Learn to use a 'clear communication tool'

Duration

One to two hours

What you'll need

- A quiet, uninterrupted space
- A clock with a second-hand

Description

This exercise is a well-known communications tool that is used, in a number of forms, in a wide variety of situations ranging from counselling and therapy to mediation and arbitration.

It works like this: Decide who is going to start the speaking part of the exercise (Partner A) and who is going to listen (Partner B). You'll swap roles later.

If you have any troubles deciding just flip a coin.

Partner A: Choose a topic. Start with something non-controversial but interesting, such as 'things I really like to do with other people'. Take two minutes (no more) and talk about the topic to your partner. Use 'I' statements. An 'I' statement is a sentence that starts with 'I' rather than 'you' or 'one' or 'it'. For example:

> 'I like to go for walks in the woods with my friend John.'

not

> 'It's nice to go for walk in the woods with John.'

This is important as it means the communication is coming directly from the person speaking and that they are 'owning' what they are saying.

When you come to the end of your topic (keep an eye on the clock!) say 'Done' or 'Finished'.

Partner B: Listen carefully, without any interruption. Try to maintain eye contact while listening. Concentrate on listening and try to remember exactly what you hear without interpreting or reacting.

When you hear the word 'Done' or 'Finished', take a second to review internally what you have heard. The idea is to focus on hearing exactly what the other person has said without judging, reacting or responding.

When you are ready, tell the other person what you have just heard. Don't add any interpretation or judgement and don't start a discussion; simply reflect back as accurately as you can. The goal is to ensure that you have heard accurately what the other person said.

When you come to the end of your 'reflection' say 'Done' or 'Finished'.

Partner A: If, after you have heard everything reflected back to you, you feel that you were not heard correctly, you can repeat what you said and ask to have it reflected again. Don't change what you've said but it's OK, if necessary, to add a small clarification.

Both Partners: Repeat the speaking/reflection process until what has been said is reflected accurately. Once an accurate reflection has taken, switch roles so that Partner B speaks and Partner A reflects.

Here's an example:

Partner A: 'I like to go for walks in the woods with my friend John.'

Partner B: ' You like to go out walking with John.'

Partner A: 'I like to go for walks in the woods with my friend John.'

Partner B: ' You like to go out walking in the woods.'

Partner A: 'I like to go for walks in the woods with my friend John.'

Partner B: 'You like to go out walking in the woods with your friend John.'

After Partner B has successfully reflected back to Partner A what she or he has said, Partner B takes two minutes to speak on the topic.

Partner A then reflects what she or he has heard with, if required, a few clarification rounds.

Do three complete rounds of Partner A speaks / Partner B reflects / Partner B speaks / Partner A reflects.

While you're doing the exercise, observe how accurately you can hear the other person. Your listening will normally become more accurate over time.

When completed successfully this exercise results in:

- The person speaking knowing that they are heard
- The person listening knowing that they have heard correctly

This is the basis of good communication. What most people discover when they do the exercise (anyway, we did) is that they don't actually hear what the other person is saying. If you've been in a relationship for a long time, you may even find that you're so sure that you know what the other person is going to say that you don't even hear what they're *actually* saying.

Once you have completed this 'accurate listening' exercise you can put it to the test. Do the exercise again and talk about:

'What really gets my sexual energy going'

The exercise itself is all about listening accurately without judgement. It's not about having a discussion although, after you're finished with the exercise, a discussion may well take place. We found that one of the most common things we talked about afterwards is how the same word, as well as the way a word was said, often meant very different things to each of us. We often find ourselves sorting out the confusion caused as a result!

The next time you find yourself arguing or getting bothered with your partner try Active Listening and see what happens.

Chapter 7

Practising

Sacred Touch

The Understanding

> The softest things in the world
> overcome the hardest things in the world.
> —Lao Tzu

To touch, and to be touched, is a great part of what sex is all about. Dual Cultivation practices teach that conscious, gentle and loving touch creates the right conditions for Sexual Qi to flow through the whole body.

Touch that is done roughly, or with disrespect, can leave psychic, emotional or physical wounds in our mind and body. It is possible to heal these wounds with Sacred Touch.

The Background

Sexual energy is powerful. The urge to procreate is the basis of life itself. Just look at the animal and plant life on our planet and you'll see how much energy is spent on making sure that the next generation can come into being. Humans are no exception to this. If you need any further confirmation, just think about how many lives, families, organisations and even empires have been altered simply because of an irresistible attraction between a man and a woman.

Humans differ from the rest of nature in one key respect, however. We have free will. We can learn to be conscious of our sexual energy and choose how to express it. Unfortunately, the way most people are taught to handle their sexual energy is to control and suppress it. When we finally feel that we are in situation where it is safe to be sexual, we are often disappointed to discover that the energy does not flow very well. It's sort of like spending a great deal of time blocking up a stream and then being surprised that there is not much water left to swim in when the time comes.

So why is there all this control and suppression around sexual energy? One answer is that it's just not acceptable, at least in most societies and in most situations, to approach an unknown person on the street and simply engage in sexual activity with them. We feel, quite correctly, that this is part of what defines civilized behaviour. There is an elaborate set of rules, both spoken and unspoken, that regulate who can have sex with whom and under what circumstances. Figuring out and applying this complicated set of rules and regulations takes up a surprising amount of humankind's energy.

'Hold on!' you may say. 'This book is about Sacred Sex and we're a couple that has decided to work with sexual energy. Surely all of these rules and regulations are not an issue since we're in an agreed sexual relationship between consenting adults?' Unfortunately, it's not as simple as that. The reality is that we create tremendous tension and blockages in our bodies and minds by trying to follow all these rules and regulations and those blockages don't disappear just because we happen to be naked in the bedroom with a sexually attractive partner. Sure, the sheer raw power of sexual energy can overcome many blockages ('I just couldn't help myself.') but what does that lead to? A rush of energy that is wonderful at the time but afterwards can leave you with a curious feeling of regret and emptiness. To go back to the stream analogy, it's almost as if the stream finally bursts through the dam holding it back and then completely floods the garden leaving a right old mess afterwards. A far cry from the steady, nourishing flow of Sexual Qi we need to keep ourselves growing and thriving.

Sacred Sex practitioners recognized this and saw that many of these blockages were based on previous unhappy experiences and that the memories of these are 'stored' in our bodies. You can see how this works with this simple experiment: just try and put your finger in the flame of a candle. Notice the hesitation? You learned at an early age that fire hurts and now you exercise great caution. So how does this work in regards to sexual energy? An example could be if your mother (or primary carer) did not like touching your genitals. As a result, you would have been given a message very early on that 'genitals are bad'. How many people have had their hands slapped as a small child when they touched their 'private parts'? Negative body experiences such as these leave their marks deep in the psyche and our body memory and are a powerful part of who we think we are and what we believe about our sexuality and ourselves.

To work successfully with Sacred Sex you need to undo this conditioning. This is where having a willing partner comes into its own. It's much, much easier to work with another person to peel away the layers of the onion of negative body conditioning than it is to do it by yourself. The good news is that our bodies are longing to be freed from the tension and stress that this negative conditioning has created. For most people it's simply a matter of slowly and gently healing the wounds by replacing those old, unhappy experiences with new, wonderful ones.

Stephan's Story

I'll be honest. Our sex life wasn't great when we started off with Sacred Sex. I was pretty frustrated both with Mieke and myself. I found out later that she was just as unhappy. It seemed that, no matter how hard I tried, I really couldn't get much energy going between us. I didn't know how to talk about it with her and I guess I just sort of hoped that somehow the sparks might fly again like they had when we met. We did have a good time once in a blue moon, as I used to say, but I could never figure out why. I certainly had no sure-fire method I could use to get the sexual energy going between us. I knew Mieke felt as bad about this as I did, but we just didn't have any way to move out of the rut we were in.

To top it off, we were stuck in what I now realize is called a 'negative feedback loop': I would show sexual interest without checking to see if she was interested first; she would not want to disappoint me and tried hard; I saw that it wasn't working and felt bad about it; she saw that I felt bad and felt worse. Great, eh? From what I've heard and read, I now understand that this sort of situation is not at all uncommon, but that's not a lot of help when you're stuck in it.

So when we started off with some of the massage and relaxation exercises, it was tough going for me. I'd never done much massage and approached it pretty much the way I approached everything; in other words, read the instructions, do the best I could and hopefully Mieke would enjoy it. It didn't help that, as usual, part of me was afraid that I would do something wrong and I was, as often, hypersensitive to anything that might sound like a whiff of criticism.

We'd reserved an evening and I started by arranging a mattress with a nice cloth on it in front of the open fire. I then put on some soft music that I had especially bought for the occasion. Mieke lay down on the mattress and I picked up the bottle of massage oil. I gently poured a bit on her back.

'Aargh!' she cried and jerked away from me. 'That's cold!'

Right, cold massage oil on a warm back is not such a great feeling. Unfortunately, I immediately went into my 'I can never do anything right' state and Mieke, noticing this, shut up completely and said precious little that evening. Oh well, so much for the relaxation and communication exercise.

The next week we tried again. Mieke, who had done quite a bit of massage and attended a course or two, chatted with me as I lit the fire. I asked her what we might have learned from last week and what we might do differently. I really was trying to learn this communication stuff. She looked at me as if to see whether I was really serious in wanting to know, and whether I would be upset if she said something. I guess I must have looked approachable and she ventured:

'You know, I learned in my course that, when you give a massage, you pour the oil into the palm of your hand and let it warm up a bit first. That way it feels really nice when you then put your hands on someone.'

Since this was not a criticism directed at me, I had no trouble hearing her and thought, 'now that's a clever idea!' This time, when I applied the oil, I got to hear 'mmmm' instead of 'aargh'. Things went much better that evening.

That probably sounds like a really simple story. But within it lay the seeds of a complete transformation in our relationship. I started to listen, and Mieke started to talk. For the previous twenty years it had usually been the other way around. Once we learned how to do this, i.e. take turns speaking and listening and really hear each other, we found that there was absolutely no problem, small or large, that we couldn't sooner our later find our way through.

So what was the difference? Instead of saying 'last week you poured cold oil on me and it was awful' she shared some information with me to help make the experience pleasant. That made all the difference in the world to me and gave me a chance to relax and realize that she, too, wanted to have a nice time and was very willing to help make the evening a success. No, this wasn't a blinding flash of transformation or inspiration, just a small shift in the way we were interacting with each other. But it did set the stage for unblocking and releasing large amounts of tension and mistrust that had accumulated over our years together.

Mieke's Story

New challenges present themselves at regular intervals during our sessions. This time the problem is with touching myself in a sexual way in front of Stephan. I have always been very shy; even as a child and teenager I would blush at the slightest look from someone I did not know very well, let alone a man! I thought I had got over this in my thirties and forties, but now I realize I am still very shy, even in front of my partner of so many years! One night we were preparing ourselves in front of the fire. I found it really difficult to touch my nipples, or any other sensitive part of myself, while Stephan was watching. Of course I had done all this before, in the privacy of my bed, or my room, when I was alone. I wondered why I felt so shy now? I don't have anything to hide! I felt really naked, vulnerable, scared even, to show this part of myself I had hidden for so long. Then I realized something important: how can I be comfortable being touched by another when I can't openly touch myself? Many thoughts and feelings go through my head! Why am I so shy to show my partner that I get sexually excited? Perhaps one explanation is that I was brought up to be a good Catholic girl, and good girls don't do such things! I thought I had grown out of all this but it just goes to show how hard it is to get rid of these old thought-forms and patterns! I decided this was silly; I don't need this childhood stuff anymore, I told myself: let it go! We are both here to learn and experiment, and have fun.

I did not change over night. Slowly I allowed myself to stimulate my nipples while Stephan was watching. Then I noticed that he became even more aroused when he was watching me, especially when I stroked my pubic area, and clitoris. I in turn became more excited, and so a dance was created between us. I had always known that men were more visually-oriented, but to experience this and play with it was new for me! I liked it; it was fun!

After this insight, our sessions changed. I often started off with stimulating myself, watching Stephan getting more aroused. It also helped him to relax more, as he no longer felt he had to do all the hard work to 'warm me up', at least in his mind.

What was happening with me? I was slowly changing the image I had of myself: I was slowly accepting that I was a sexy woman, and enjoyed myself, that I allowed myself to show this, that it gave me pleasure. Yes, I'm responsible for my own sexuality. I'm in charge; I don't always need to wait for someone else to give me pleasure!

The Tension Release Exercise

Goals

- Free up tension in your body with non-sexual massage
- Learn how to communicate positively about physical sensation

Duration

One to two hours

Note: Powerful feelings and emotions can be released, sometimes quite unexpectedly, when you start to work with touch. This is normal and totally OK. You don't have to do anything at all except 'be there' for your partner while he or she is experiencing the emotions or feelings. You don't have to 'fix' it or make it better. If asked, hold your partner in a gentle embrace. The feelings will pass. It's very healing.

What you'll need to create your 'Sacred Sex Space'

- A peaceful, warm space – ideally not your bedroom.
- You may want to invest in a mattress and washable cover for your ongoing exercises and 'Sacred Sex' time.
- Some nice music (see the Reference section for suggestions), candles and/or incense and any other thing you feel will create a special atmosphere.
- Some massage oil in a small bowl. Unscented almond oil is ideal; however, your local health-food shop will certainly have a range to choose from.
- Some towels that are OK to get oily, as you'll need to wash them afterwards.
- A small clock with a second-hand.

Description

It doesn't matter if you have never given a massage before, as the purpose of the exercise is not about working with muscles or even stimulating any particular part of the body. If you discover, as we did, that massage is a crucial part of getting your sexual energy going, you may want to do an introductory course or buy some 'how-to' books or videos to learn more about different techniques. Most people do just fine 'going with flow', however. The most important thing, as you will soon see, is communication.

Decide from the beginning whether you wish to be totally naked or not. This exercise is not about becoming sexually excited. We are all different when it comes to our level of comfort with being naked and how much the sight of a naked body gets our sexual energy going. If you find that you 'just can't help yourself' in the presence of a beautiful, naked man or woman, then a light wrap might help keep proceedings cooler.

I suggest you begin all of your practice sessions with a Greeting Ritual. This is a very simple, ancient practice that simply means taking time to see, acknowledge and honour each other. Sacred Sex is all about creating the physical, emotional and psychic space and conditions for sexual energy flow. If this sounds all a bit 'airy-fairy' then look at it another way. It's pretty cool that you've got someone who's willing to try this Sacred Sex stuff out with you, right? There's nothing wrong with saying a small 'Thank You for Being Here' before getting started, is there?

Sample Dialogue

Here's a suggestion for how to do this:

Sit down facing each other. Take a moment just to hold each other's gaze before one of you says something like:

'Thank you for being here with me right now. I really look forward to learning about Sacred Sex with you. You're great!'

The other person responds:

'It's nice to be here. I'm a bit nervous but there's nobody else I'd rather be naked and nervous with. I love you, too!'

Be real. You don't have to come up with deep, meaningful expressions of undying devotion to the God and Goddess within each other. By all means, feel free to do so if the Spirit moves you. What we discovered was that it was the fact that we took the time simply to appreciate each other and acknowledge that we were spending some special time together that made all the difference. Sometimes all that was needed was a simple deep look and a 'Thank You'.

Now it's time for the hands-on practice. First, decide who is to start as the Giver and who is going to be the Receiver for the first round. You'll swap places later. If you can't decide you can always flip a coin!

Receiver: Lie down on the mattress on your stomach and get comfortable. Make sure you are warm enough.

Giver: Move to one side.

Now remind your partner that this is a feedback-based massage. Tell your partner that he or she will be asked for regular positive and directional feedback, and that you will adjust what you are doing as a result.

Sample Dialogue

Giver: *In this exercise you, The Receiver, are in complete control. I am here to serve you and to discover what you enjoy and appreciate while being touched.*

I'm going to start by gently touching you on your back. Please give me positive, instructive feedback on a regular basis. I need to know:

> • *Does it feel good exactly where I am touching you or should I move somewhere else?*
>
> • *Is my stroke long/short/strong/gentle enough?*
>
> • *Is there someway I can adjust what I am doing to be more pleasurable or is it just right the way it is?*
>
> *If you don't say anything at all I will ask you on a regular basis just to make sure. Please use positive statements. Even if something isn't quite right, try to phrase your feedback in a way that is easy for me to hear and that appreciates that I'm doing my best.*
>
> *It's OK to make nice noises.*

Giver: Before you start the actual massage, see if you can create a space of 'unknowing' in yourself. Consider the following thought:

'I may think I know this person that I am about to touch but I'm open to the possibility that there is much that I do not know. I'd like to find out from him or her directly what he or she enjoys and try to learn how to give exactly what he or she wants.'

Now ask your partner to tell you of any particular places that he or she might like to have some attention paid to, such as a stiff shoulder or tense lower back. Then, take some oil in your palm, let it warm up a bit and gently place your hands on the small of the Receiver's back. Gently move in small circles to spread the oil out, up and down the back. Now move into performing a single movement. This could be a stroke or a gentle kneading action, whatever you like. As soon as you've gotten into the rhythm of the movement and have repeated it four or five times, ask for some feedback.

Receiver: Give positive feedback when asked. Most likely you'll find that it will take a few questions and answers back and forth to find out which particular stroke is just right.

Positive Feedback Sample Dialogue

What is positive feedback? It's when you give someone information in a way that encourages them and supports them, even when you give information that could be perceived as criticism. An example of this is the difference between:

> 'That's not nice. Can you do something else?'
>
> *and*
>
> 'Hmm, thanks, but could you move up and
> massage my shoulder a bit?'
>
> *The difference is that you accentuate the positive and give clear instructions as to how to proceed to make the experience better. It can be quite disheartening to hear negative feedback (and a mood-killer as well) and it's also much more efficient to tell someone what they can do to be successful rather than just tell them that they are a failure. Most people realize this, of course, but sometimes there are old, criticism-based feedback patterns that are hard to break.*

Giver: Once you've settled into something that works, just keep at it. Don't change or stop unless, of course, The Receiver asks you to. Now, have a look at the clock and make a note of the position of the second hand. If after sixty seconds there has been no sound or statement, check in with The Receiver. If, after five minutes, you're still on the same stroke, you can mention that you're going to move to a new area and ask, again, if there is any place in particular that needs attention. The process of asking and listening as you touch is an important part of this exercise, as it builds trust.

> *Note on Arousal*
>
> *If you discover that Sexual Qi is being aroused (even though the Giver should attempt to steer clear of any specifically sexual touch), say so. If the Receiver communicates that Sexual Qi is being aroused, it is an opportunity for the Giver to:*
>
> • *Note the spot/stroke for future reference*
> • *Slowly pull back from what you are doing*

Giver: Carry on with the massage and feedback. A neat tip that Mieke taught me is always to keep one hand touching the Receiver. So, if you want to move from one side of the Receiver's body to the other, you simply keep one hand lightly resting on the Receiver's back. This keeps the connection and avoids the shock of having a hand suddenly placed somewhere else on their body.

The real exercise is to learn how to communicate about touch and sensation. This exercise touches on many of the fundamentals of Sacred Sex: trust, respect, communication, sensitivity and safety.

After fifteen minutes (or longer, but no longer than half an hour) it's time for the Receiver to turn over. First, take a towel and wipe down their back and then let them turn over in their own time. If they have really relaxed they might even have dozed off a bit. You can gently wake them by gently dragging the tops of your fingers up and down their back.

Now continue with up to half an hour of massage on the front of the body, the same way as you did on the back. Most people are a bit more sensitive around their stomach and chest areas so you will want to proceed gently and cautiously. At the end of the front massage, wipe the Receiver down with a towel again.

Receiver: At this point, you might wish to give the Giver a hug and a 'Thank You' for all the love and attention that you have been given.

Now it's time to reverse roles as Giver becomes Receiver and Receiver becomes Giver.

At the end of the exercise, take a moment to sit quietly for a second and feel how nice it is to be relaxed and comfortable in each other's company.

We've discovered that regular massages, even very short ones like a little shoulder rub, have made a huge difference to the energy flow between us.

Chapter 8

Circulating Qi

The Understanding

> It is elusive and evasive,
> yet it does manifest itself.
> —Lao Tzu

When you circulate your Sexual Qi throughout your entire body, you open up channels for the flow of orgasmic energy. This allows you to experience multiple, powerful and healing whole-body orgasms. Using this circulation technique, you can safely increase the amount of Sexual Qi that flows through your body.

The Background

Qi is a fundamental Taoist term for life-force or the spiritual energy that is part of everything that exists. Working with Qi forms the basis of all the Taoist practices that involve understanding the flow of energy, whether it be acupuncture, martial arts, feng shui or Dual Cultivation. Yet the existence of Qi has not been proven in any familiar, Western sense of the word. Even within Taoism and Chinese culture, there have been heated debates as to the nature of Qi. In the West, there have been people – for example, Wilhelm Reich – who attempted to work with Qi-like energies such as 'orgone'. Yet none of these attempts have been accepted by the Western scientific community.

But Dual Cultivation is all about working with Qi. This can, understandably, be a source of confusion and possibly an obstacle if you're the sort of person who has to have intellectual proof of something before proceeding to invest a lot of time and effort in it. If so, you have my heartfelt compassion since that description fits me pretty well! The only reason I was willing to try working with Qi was the fact that it is a cornerstone of practices that have been in existence for thousands of years, and many of these practices clearly work. Few can doubt the incredible results obtained by martial artists and acupuncture has been clinically demonstrated to work. The way I got around this mental block was to, quite simply, accept that Qi stands for something that I don't totally understand and then accept that I don't need to understand everything!

After much research, what I did see clearly was that you don't need to see, feel or understand Qi in order to be able to start with the Dual Cultivation practices. Most of the practices concentrate not on *understanding* Qi, but rather on *cultivating* Qi. The Qi cultivation process is often described as a combination of repetitive movements, concentration and breathing. Over time, a sense of Qi flow emerges when you follow the steps carefully and consistently. Different people experience it in different ways. Some experience warmth, some experience tingling in their hands and feet and some just report an inner sense of peace and grounding. Now, whether that sense of Qi is just 'getting the hang of it', 'a useful way to describe a state where you are more aware of what is happening inside yourself' or indeed 'an awareness of Qi' is, in my experience, immaterial. Everyone I have spoken to who has persevered with a Taoist practice, whether Qi Gong, Tai Chi or Dual Cultivation, has clearly felt that 'something is happening' and that whatever that 'something' is, it's reproducible. Since the Taoists have a handy term for that 'something', *i.e.* Qi, it makes sense to use it.

As you do the exercises, it's totally normal in the beginning to feel that not much is happening when it comes to 'Qi sensing'. Just keep practising on a regular basis and you will observe how you become aware of Qi flowing and how you can use this awareness to manage your Sexual Qi. By learning techniques to work with Qi, you can accomplish many things that are just not possible using Western understandings of the body and life-energy.

So what does the statement in the **Understanding** 'safely increase the amount of Sexual Qi you move through your body' mean? Imagine for a second that you applied a 100 amp electrical current to a circuit that was rated at only 3 amps. What would happen? If there were a fuse, you would blow it: if there were no fuse, you could start a fire or damage some equipment on the same circuit. Our body/mind system is no different. A severe Qi overload in the brain is called a 'Kundalini Psychosis' and it can lead to a delusional state. In my observation, less severe overload can create a state of being quite ungrounded and slightly delirious after a good dose of Sexual Qi that has not been handled wisely. It's good fun but, unfortunately, the effect does not last long and the let-down afterwards can be quite severe and be accompanied by feelings of depression and listlessness. That is why it's a really good idea to learn how to circulate Sexual Qi before learning how to generate it. That way you've put circuits into place to handle the flow once it starts. It makes a lot of sense if you think about it.

Stephan's Story

When Mieke and I started working with Dual Cultivation practices, one of the books we used was 'Cultivating Female Sexual Energy' by Mantak Chia. Being the enthusiast that I am, I read hastily through the beginning of the book (most of which made no sense to me at the time) and suggested to Mieke that we start with one of the 'Traditional Love-making Exercises for Healing' towards the end of the book.

There was a position detailed in one chapter that was specifically designed to help with the healing of all the internal organs and that was exactly what we needed. There are also some nice, Chinese line-drawings in the book that show quite clearly what to do. The instructions were clear as well: you are supposed to practise up to four sets of nine strokes, four times per day, for fifteen days. The man is also not supposed to ejaculate at all when doing the exercises.

'Right,' I thought. 'This seems easy enough.' So that evening we gave it a try. We laid down on our sides facing each other, Mieke moved her legs back as shown in the drawing and I started off with my four sets of nine strokes. Except that I didn't make it. The first nine went fine and the break in between was great as I managed to cool down a bit. I made it half way through the second set of nine strokes; Mieke wiggled just a little bit and then ejaculation time arrived. After that my erection disappeared, as was always the case with me after an ejaculation.

Mieke was very understanding. 'I'm sure we'll do better next time,' she said, encouragingly.

So the next morning we tried again. This time she was very attentive and did her very best not to move at all since that clearly was very stimulating for me and not at all helpful when it came to my attempts not to ejaculate. This time I managed two and a half sets. Oh well, better but not quite what I had hoped for.

We tried again that evening. When I sensed I was nearing 'the point of no return', I stopped moving altogether. I still ejaculated after a few seconds even though we were both lying still. Aargh! The next morning we tried with the same result. Double aargh! I was just not managing to make it through the four times nine without ejaculating. This was frustrating. I'd actually never paid any attention at all to trying to manage myself in such a way that I would delay or avoid ejaculating and I was amazed at how difficult it was proving to be.

So, somewhat chastened and feeling a bit humbler, I went back to the books. This time I had a look in the other book by Mantak Chia that I had bought, called 'Cultivating Male Sexual Energy'. Lots of it still didn't make much sense, but I understood more of it than the first time I had read it. When I got to the chapter on 'The Secrets of Semen Retention', I slowed right down and read every word carefully. In the section titled 'The Importance of the Small or Microcosmic Orbit' I saw that what was described was exactly what I was experiencing. While we were practising, my sexual energy was getting hotter and hotter until finally it was finding the fastest way out it could which, not surprisingly, was through ejaculation.

The book explains that it is possible to do something about this by using the Small Orbit to draw the energy away from the genital area and up into the rest of the body. What you're supposed to do is squeeze your PC muscles (just as if you are trying to stop yourself peeing in mid-stream) and visualize energy being pulled up your spine. If you can do this you can catch yourself before you ejaculate and draw the energy upwards instead. It sounded like it was worth a try and, if it worked, it would be a big help to our exercises!

Before our next exercise session, I told Mieke about this Orbit I had read about and explained that I wanted to try it. I told her that, if I had understood it correctly, it would help if she, too, would imagine the energy being pulled upwards at the same time as I was squeezing my PC muscles.

So off we went as before. In the middle of the third set of nine I sensed I was nearing 'the point of no return'. This time I looked at Mieke, squeezed my PC muscle, took a deep breath and pulled the energy upwards. Success at last! The urge to ejaculate subsided and was replaced with the feeling of a warm glow throughout my body. It seems the Taoists knew what they were talking about after all.

Mieke's Story

Stephan is great. He is always full of ideas and wants to work on exciting projects. Life with him is never boring! Some of these projects are just 'brainchildren'; they don't grow up. But others do and become real, such as this idea about working with sexual energy to heal. At first, I must say, I had my suspicions. Was this another hare-brained scheme of his? Before saying 'Yes', I thought about it. I'm interested in healing, in herbal remedies, in being self-sufficient and in taking charge of my own healing. I come from the back-to-nature movement of the 1970s. Most importantly, I'm always curious and willing to try new things. So I said 'Yes' to this plan of his.

After a few months of our new adventure, 'working with sexual energy for healing', I was feeling less enthusiastic. I wondered why I was doing this. Nothing much had happened. Our sessions by the fire followed similar patterns. We were learning to talk more openly and honestly about things that mattered in our relationship but I didn't feel much change in myself and I didn't seem to have a lot more energy.

Stephan was working really hard at it. He was incredibly patient and persevering, stubborn even. He really wanted this to work for me. If I was honest with myself I, on the other hand, was getting a little bit sceptical. But most importantly I felt bad about Stephan's trying so hard. I love him and I was touched by what he wanted to do for me and by what he wanted to change in himself! What about me? I realized I had not fully said YES. The day this insight came to me I told myself: YES! I have nothing to lose here, things can only get better, and I will do my part of the work. I will concentrate, as it takes two to tango! I felt that, up to then, I had said 'Yes' for a lot of reasons but I never said 'Yes' to myself. I had to give myself permission to be open and relaxed. I didn't say this to Stephan; I just said it quietly to myself.

Our next session started off as usual. Stephan gave me a lovely Yoni massage. My breathing was much deeper and more relaxed. I could let go. I did my Qi circulation and I got very excited. Then he was kissing me. Stephan's really good with his tongue! I love it. Suddenly there was a big white flash of light: it came out of my sacrum and made a big loop in the air to connect with my navel! I was so surprised. I felt a little light-headed. Stephan saw the flash too and he got a slight headache. We spent quite a long time just lying in each other's arms, very still, in awe of what we had just experienced. After some time, I told Stephan that I had said YES! He just nodded. For once he didn't have much to say.

So what happened? I had been practising the microcosmic orbit on my own; I knew I could move the energy up my spine. And I knew that the energy moving down the front was not quite making it, until that day. The circuit was complete! It had everything to do with saying 'Yes' to myself. This was a very important experience for me. It is about taking responsibility for yourself and not only for your sexual energy. If you say 'Yes' in this way, blockages are overcome. Ever since that day, thinking back about what happened helps me to overcome difficulties in other situations too.

The Small Orbit Exercise

Please do not skip over this exercise. The Small Orbit is a fundamental tool for directing Sexual Qi. If you do not use it when practising Dual Cultivation, you can end up with uncomfortable and unpleasant side-effects due to ungrounded Qi.

Goals

- Learn how the Small Orbit works
- Practise directing your Sexual Qi through the Small Orbit
- Learn how to store Sexual Qi in your Tan Tien

Duration

Fifteen minutes

Note: You can learn this exercise by yourself as it does not require a partner.

Description

Find a peaceful, undisturbed time and space. A good time is early morning before the rush of the day starts.

Relax. Meditate (still your mind) for a few minutes. Now curl your tongue so that the tip of your tongue touches the roof of your mouth. In this position your tongue acts as a 'circuit-breaker' that connects the energy channel that flows up your spine with the energy channel that flows down the front of your body.

Now use your mind to trace an energy circuit in your body. The circuit starts at your Hui Yin. The Hui Yin is the point between your legs half way between your Yoni/Jade Stalk and your anus. This is also called the perineum in Western medicine, whilst in acupuncture it is point CV 1. Follow along the circuit in your mind as it goes up your spine to the top of your head, down the centre of your forehead to the roof of your mouth, through your tongue, down your throat and the centre of your chest and navel and then back down to the perineum. Do this nine times.

The trick to the exercise is to follow the energy with your mind as it flows around. I found that, if I imagined a little white ball of light (a Qi Ball) that I followed as it travelled around, I could begin to sense the flow. In the Taoist practice

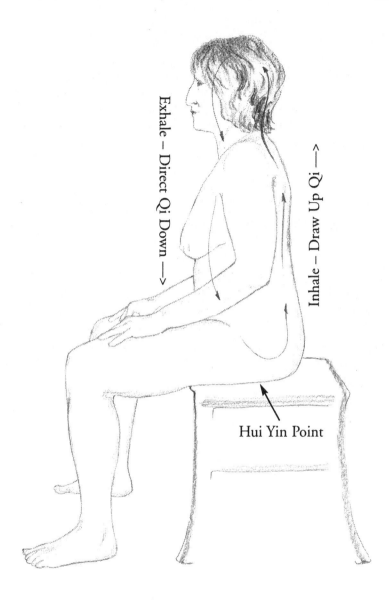

Exhale – Direct Qi Down —>

Inhale – Draw Up Qi —>

Hui Yin Point

of Qi Gong (translation: 'Energy Cultivation' or 'Working with Energy'), there is a saying that 'Where the Mind Goes, Qi Flows'. In other words, the very fact that you are using your mind to imagine an energy circuit actually creates one.

Next, synchronize your breathing with the flow. When the Qi Ball is at your Hui Yin, take a slow, deep breath. As you inhale, watch the Qi Ball as it travels up the spine. When the Qi Ball reaches the top of your head, start to exhale and watch it travel down the front channel until it reaches its starting point. Do this nine times.

Finally, learn how to give the Qi Ball a push by closing and squeezing your Hui Yin. To push the Qi Ball you inhale, give your PC muscle a squeeze and push the Qi Ball up your spine. Your PC muscle is the muscle you use when you stop yourself peeing in mid-stream. It's also the same muscle that women learn to use when they practise Kegel exercises to strengthen their pelvic floor. Again, do the circuit nine times. Remember to keep the tip of your tongue up and touching the roof of your mouth when practising Qi circulation.

At the end of your Qi circulation session, you can pack or store the energy you have generated and circulated by mentally directing it to your Lower Tan Tien or Elixir Field. This is a point in the body located behind and slightly below the navel. This point is also called the Hara in Japanese. It is the balance point of your body. If you lean past the point moving forward, gravity will start to pull your body forward, and vice versa for backwards. So the point is inside your body.

To collect Sexual Qi in the Tan Tien, circulate your Qi as described above. As the Qi Ball makes its way down the front of your body, direct it with your mind so that it stops at your Tan Tien. Place your hands over your Tan Tien. You may even feel some heat in your palms when you do this. Breathe deeply for a minute or two and relax your body while visualizing the Qi ball spiralling around your Tan Tien and finally coming to rest in it.

When you're finished, you can shake your hands away from the sides of your body. This will disperse any excess Qi that wasn't stored in the Tan Tien. If, for any reason, you experience negative or unpleasant feelings when the Small Orbit is completed, simply visualize the negative energy leaving your body as grey smoke. Imagine that the grey smoke exits from your hands and feet and returns to the Earth for 're-cycling'. This is a handy tool that you can use any time you wish to get rid of negative emotions or feelings.

Once you've learned the Small Orbit you can practise putting it to use. All you need to do is get some Sexual Qi going and then pull the energy up your spine. A straightforward way of doing this for men is self-stimulation of the Jade Stalk while taking great care not to go beyond the 'point of no return'. For women, manually massaging the breasts and/or clitoris or even using a vibrator can do the trick. Just get some Sexual Qi going, stop stimulating yourself and then immediately pull the Sexual Qi around your circuit. Do this three, six or nine times and then store the generated Qi in your Tan Tien.

You can practise the Small Orbit anywhere; standing in a queue at the bank, watching TV, in the middle of a business meeting – all are places where circulat-ing your Qi can be of great benefit (although getting the *Sexual* Qi going in pub-lic is inadvisable!). You will find after a time that the Small Orbit has a deeply calming effect on your body, your mind and your emotions.

Chapter 9

Yoni Massage

The Understanding

> Nature does not hurry,
> yet everything is accomplished.
> —Lao Tzu

Women can learn how to manage and direct their flow of Sexual Qi. Men can help women create a safe space in which to do this by acting as a respectful and communicative partner. The Yoni Massage is a tool that couples can use to create the right setting and conditions that make it easier for women to say 'Yes!' to their Sexual Qi flow.

The Background

The Yoni Massage is a wonderful opportunity for men to learn more about how women's, and specifically their partner's, Sexual Qi works in a very practical, hands-on fashion. It also offers a setting for women to get more in touch with their Sexual Qi, lower barriers to its flow and to experience an intimate, deep connection with the man giving the Yoni Massage.

During a Yoni Massage a man:

- Helps a woman pull her Sexual Qi up from her Hui Yin towards the clitoris and then towards the heart. This helps a woman to connect her Sexual Qi with the rest of her being and begins to open up the channels for Sexual Qi to flow through.

- 'Warms the Oven'. This comes from the Chinese saying: 'You can't bake bread in a cold oven.' In other words, if you want to generate Sexual Qi, you get the best results if the stove, i.e. the woman's sexual organs, are warmed up and aroused before engaging in sexual activity.

- Demonstrates to the woman physically, emotionally and mentally that he is present, responsive and aware of her. For many women this is an incredible aphrodisiac. I recently heard some feedback from women who had had their first encounter with a trained, male, Sacred Sex adept. I was curious to know what aspect of the sexual delights they had experienced made the biggest impression. Surprisingly, it had nothing to do with the sex at all. It was the fact that these men gave the women their full, undivided attention that made such an impression. The men involved were completely, 100% present and focused on the desires and wishes of the women they were with.

During the Yoni Massage a woman:

- Learns to circulate her Sexual Qi as it is being aroused.
- Practises staying fully present and connected to her partner while experiencing Sexual Qi flow.
- Learns to relax and allow Sexual Qi to flow through her entire body and practises techniques to release tensions and blockages that impede its free flow.

Finally, what a couple learns during the Yoni Massage is how to work together to bring forth Sexual Qi consciously and openly by communicating clearly with each other and saying 'Yes'.

Stephan's Story

I was never taught how to touch a woman as, unfortunately, they didn't have that course at any of the schools I attended. Instead, I learned through observation of family, friends and what I saw on TV and at the movies. Later, in my teens, I learned through a trial-and-error process with my girlfriends.

I did try my best but, quite frankly, I really didn't know what I was doing. I suppose it's a small consolation that none of my friends did either but that didn't do a lot of good for the girls at the receiving end of my attentions. It was clear to me, although you wouldn't have gotten me to admit it out loud, that I didn't really know how to 'give a woman an orgasm' but, on the other hand, neither did I know how to remedy that lack of education.

When Mieke and I first met I had already had a bit of sexual experience. None of it had been all that great. I guess I was a bit uptight and could never really relax enough just to enjoy myself. When Mieke and I fell madly in love, the rush of endorphins was a great aphrodisiac. Even though my skills weren't any better, it was wonderful to make love with someone I was so totally in love with. Unfortunately, like so many other couples, that falling in love energy lasted for just a few years before it slowly but surely started to fade away. Our sex-life faded as well, especially as the children took up more and more of our time. This, too, is an all-too-familiar story that I've heard from other couples.

We had been together for just over twenty years when Mieke fell ill and my sexual esteem was pretty much non-existent at that point. I felt that Mieke had no sexual interest in me at all and that if I touched her in any sort of a sexual way it really didn't matter to her and certainly didn't excite her. It turns out that this wasn't actually true but it's what I felt at the time. It wasn't that we didn't have a sex-life, it's just that it was pretty low in energy. More like a nice cuddle rather than lots of orgasmic energy. We loved each other but there wasn't a lot of sexual spark between us. I had resigned myself to this and pretty much given up hope of ever changing it.

When Mieke said 'Yes' to working with Sacred Sex to try and heal her illness, I was totally amazed. It's not just that she was ill and had no energy, it's that I really didn't believe she would want to do that with me. It took a while to sink in but, when it did, I realized that there might, just, be a small chance that something might happen to that lack of sexual energy between us. Yes, it was primarily Mieke's health I was concerned about, but I also hoped that working with Sacred Sex practices might do something for our relationship as well. I really had no idea what might happen, though.

As I read through the books I had bought all those years ago, I soon realized that I had some serious homework to do. There were a lot of exercises to perform alone and some of the couple exercises appeared to have little to do with sex. I still remember our children laughing as I tried to use my tongue to move an orange that I had strung up on piece of string in the doorway as a 'tongue strengthening' exercise. I guess they always thought their Dad was crazy but this probably confirmed it!

One of the very first exercises we did together was the Yoni massage. This was something brand new for me. I had never spent a lot of time examining or massaging a woman's sexual organs before. I followed the instructions carefully and discovered that I actually quite enjoyed the gentle, quiet and relaxed time we spent before the fire. To start with, there was very little Sexual Qi flowing but this was OK, as I had no idea what to expect or what would happen. But, slowly but surely over the months, Mieke started to relax more and more and became excited. This was really, really nice for me. For the first time in my life I felt like I was allowed to touch a woman and she was enjoying it and even asking for more! I realize now that the communication and trust we built up over those many months was crucial to Mieke's healing process and my growth as a skilled lover. It's never too late to learn.

Mieke's Story

Stephan thought I was not interested in having sex with him. I thought he was not really keen to have sex with me. When he tried to touch me in a sexual way, I was often too tired, or preoccupied with kids or work. We had grown apart and the spark was not there anymore. It's not that I did not want to, and I still loved him very much; it's that we were stuck in a rut and I did not know how to get out of it. It was much easier to have sexual energy with someone new, someone with whom I did not have many years' history. I also knew I could have sexual energy by myself. I had experienced this on several occasions; being out in nature, in special places, I could get orgasms just standing with my feet firmly planted on the ground.

Many years ago, before our sex-life started slowing down, I had this longing for something else: to be able to spend more time at foreplay, to have long, slow sex, more intimate and emotional. I do remember trying to talk to Stephan about this. I remember telling him: slow down! I always had the feeling he did not know what I was talking about, and after a while I gave up. Maybe it was just a romantic notion I had. I knew what I did not want: a quickie before going to bed, then fall asleep, or fast and furious, and then suddenly it was all over. It always left me feeling irritable and unhappy.

So now we are doing Yoni massages, we are arranging Sacred Sex sessions, taking plenty of time; an old dream come true! We make a true heart connection, the whole body is involved, and it's slow! It took me some time to get used to it. I discovered it's not always easy to receive! I was just not used to it. I had spent many years of my life giving, thinking about other people, not just the family, making sure people around me were looked after. So here I was, being asked to be with myself, to be present, to communicate my feelings and what it was I liked, and even to ask for what I wanted! Oh dear, I took a deep breath and tried. My mind wandered, it was too slow, it was boring! I suddenly remembered the things I needed to add to my shopping list, etc. I did not do very well in the beginning, but Stephan was so patient, and encouraging, that after a while I got the hang of it. Concentrating on breathing and taking slow deep breaths was a great help. I started feeling muscles in my thighs I did not know I had. My muscles were not used to being touched in this way either. The massage of inner lips, clitoris and G-spot were also new sensations to me. I was starting to relax more, and so I could enjoy it more. I felt as if my whole pubic area was opening up, becoming alive again, becoming an important part of my body. Because the massage was slow, I was able to be with the feelings, and take them inside; I was not rushing ahead, because I did not really know what to expect. It was all so new and exciting!

Yoni Massage Exercise

Goals

- Create Sexual Qi through giving and receiving a Yoni massage
- Practise communicating while sexually excited

Duration

One to two hours

What you'll need

Your Sacred Sex Space together with your oil and your music etc. By the end of the book you'll probably have a complete Sacred Sex box with all of your bits and pieces!

Lots of clean towels.

You may also want to buy some water-based lubricant. We really like Liquid Silk (you can order it online) but there are others that also work well. If you and your partner use condoms, make sure you always use water-based lubricant as Latex does not like oil. Using condoms is a good idea until you have both made sure you are free of STDs and, if you are not in a monogamous relationship, you should always practise safe sex.

The man needs to make sure that he has clean hands and trimmed fingernails with no loose skin.

The woman might want to take a shower beforehand to feel clean and relaxed.

Description

In the Yoni Massage the woman is the Receiver and the man is the Giver. Yoni is the Sanskrit term for the female sexual organs. I like the word 'Yoni' as it has such a nice, soft feel to it – just like a Yoni.

This exercise has a long, detailed description and is divided into seven stages. I suggest you read all the way through it first before actually starting. At the end of the description is a quick reference that summarizes the entire massage.

STAGE 1: GATHERING THE QI

The Taoists observed that a woman's Sexual Qi is diffused through her whole body. This means that to get a woman's Sexual Qi flowing you need to 'gather' the energy in her body from her extremities towards her centre.

Both partners: Start your session with the Greeting Ritual. If you want you can extend the ritual with a short meditation. To do this, you sit facing each other, close your eyes, and still your minds. The idea is to stop thinking for a minute and simply be present. One excellent way to do this is to focus on your breathing. If you can slow your breathing down and deepen your breaths so that they come from your belly, that is even better. As you sit you'll notice that you become calmer and more present. After a few minutes (two or three is fine to start with) one partner or the other lightly squeezes the other's hand. If you're unsure as to who should do the squeezing you can agree ahead of time.

Woman: Lie down on your stomach and make yourself comfortable. Put a cushion under your head if you prefer. Relax. Breath slowly and deeply from your belly. Let your attention flow out of your head and into your body.

Man: Take fifteen minutes or so and give your partner a 'Gathering the Qi' warm-up massage. One way of doing this is to imagine that your partner has a very fine layer of gold dust covering her entire body. Your job is to gather every bit of the dust into a little heap that sits on the triangle at the base of her spine. Work slowly and methodically. Some of the dust may be a bit 'stuck' so you may have to release it gently with a bit of massage as you move along. First, do this on the back of your partner's body and then gently turn her over and collect the gold dust on the front of her body into a little pile on top of her Yoni.

Woman: During the Gathering the Qi exercise you may feel that your body begins to sensitize and even tingle a bit. Breathe into any part of your body that starts to awaken in this way. 'Breathe into' means that you take a deep breath and when you exhale you direct your attention to a specific area of your body. This helps you to relax and open.

You can gently circulate your Qi if you feel that you are becoming at all aroused.

STAGE 2: HONOUR YOUR PARTNER AND CONNECT THE CIRCUIT

According to Taoist energy-work theory, what we think and feel is just as important, if not more so, than what we do. Sexual Qi can be a raw, blasting force or it can be a gentle, subtle and yet incredibly powerful surge. The difference between the two manifestations of Sexual Qi is totally up to you and your partner's thoughts, attitudes and actions. Respect, honour, tenderness and gentleness are the key qualities to remember. These qualities, in our experience, need to be in place before the sexual touching starts.

Man: Begin by ensuring your partner is comfortable. Have lots of cushions and a light blanket available so you can cover her if she gets chilled. You may also need some cushions for under your elbows. A few of them may get oily and you might want to use pillowcases on them that you can wash later on. Place some clean towels under your partner's lower body. Move into the position as illustrated below and ensure that your partner has her head and shoulders up high enough to be able to look at you without having to bend her neck.

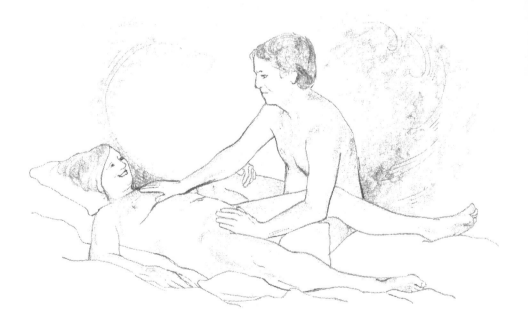

Start by making sure your hands are nice and warm by rubbing your palms vigorously together. Now 'honour' the woman by gently placing one hand on her heart (the space between her breasts) and the other gently over her Yoni. Use slow, gentle movements at all times. Look into each other's eyes while you synchronize your breathing with your partner.

Now imagine that you have an electrical circuit that starts in the palm of your left hand, runs up your left arm, through your left shoulder, across to your right shoulder, down your right arm and to the palm of your right hand. Complete this circuit by imagining that your right palm connects to your left palm through your partner's body. In other words let the flow of energy move between your hands. This helps your partner's heart connect with her Yoni. The flow direction is important as some Taoist texts indicate that you should always use your right hand to send energy and your left hand to receive it.

Hold this position for a few minutes until you both feel fully connected with each other.

Woman: It's perfectly OK and helpful to wiggle your hips or pelvis a bit to loosen up your spine while being held this way as this helps to relax the body.

Man: Stop for a second and observe the situation. Your partner is in a very vulnerable position. She's on her back, her legs are parted and you're holding her in a very intimate way. This is a Gift. This is really quite a special offering that you are privileged to receive. Just pause for a second and let that sink in inside yourself.

Woman: Stay present and aware of your body. If there is any tension in your body, keep breathing into it to help it to relax. Keep regular eye contact with your partner.

STAGE 3: LEG AND THIGH MASSAGE

Most women do not like to be grabbed or touched quickly on their sexual organs without prior warning. This is different from men who usually don't mind at all if you just reach out and touch their Jade Stalk. Instead, it's important to work in gradually towards Yoni almost as if Yoni is a gate that needs to be gently unlocked from the inside before it opens.

Man: Move both of your hands down and start to gently massage the thighs and upper legs of your partner, keeping both hands in contact with your partner's body at all times. Try to sense where any tension or stiffness might be and give a little bit of gentle extra attention to try and loosen up any knots. Tip: to loosen up a knot, it's better to repeat one gentle stroke twenty times than to give a single hard squeeze. It's important that you use movements that are relaxing and soothing at all times. Watch your partner's face even when she has her eyes closed. If she winces or frowns, that's a pretty good indication that you need to be a bit gentler. Continue massaging for five minutes or so or until you feel that her legs and thighs are loose and relaxed.

Woman: If your partner does something that is uncomfortable, give positive, directional feedback. The massage is all about generating nice, pleasant sensations. You can help your partner do this by telling him exactly what you need.

STAGE 4: APPROACH YONI AND ASK PERMISSION

Why would a man ask for permission to touch his partner, especially if they are in a long-term, committed relationship? Well, many women have had less-than-respectful experiences of men touching their bodies. This can have taken the form of unwanted or uninvited sexual touching or touch that was too hard or rough. It also happens that a woman wants to be touched but has not been completely clear about exactly what is, and what is not, OK. The man proceeds, does the 'wrong' thing and both the man and the woman end up feeling unhappy and less trusting.

One way to undo the damage that these kinds of experiences have created is for a man to demonstrate, clearly and openly, that he respects the women he is with. Asking for permission is a pretty unequivocal way of doing this. A simple but powerful acknowledgement and invitation from a woman is also, for many men, quite a wonderful experience. Certainly for me, after years of thinking incorrectly that Mieke didn't really like me touching her, it was a revolutionary step. There is power in words, and power in a clear, open and committed 'Yes'. What this exchange does is gives the woman a chance to say 'Yes'.

This also gives her the chance to say 'could I have bit more leg massage first, please?' or 'I think that's enough for this session. Maybe we could wait for the next one to go further. I would like that.' It's very important when a woman does say 'Yes' that she means it. This exercise is all about building trust at a very deep level both between a man and a woman and inside each one of them as well.

So how do you build trust in a body? As mentioned above, many women have at some time in their life experienced sexual touching in a way that was not relaxed and enjoyable. As a result, what can be called 'protective armour' has been created in the muscles around their Yonis, which actually de-sensitizes the entire area. When a man approaches Yoni with gentleness and respect he is telling his partner's body that 'things are different now, you can relax and allow yourself to feel'.

Once she starts to relax and trust, he can begin to tease forth Sexual Qi. The idea is not to stimulate a woman strongly and have Sexual Qi blast through but instead to let it build gently. The end result is, amazingly enough, a far stronger and sustained generation of Sexual Qi than would be achieved by simply applying strong stimulation directly to the clitoris. Many men find this difficult to do as they may find that they are goal-oriented and wanting to 'get on with it'. I found that if I played a little game with myself called 'Twice as Long, Half as Much' it worked wonders. What you do is, after each stroke or touch, you see if you can make the following stroke twice as long in duration and using half the pressure. The next stroke is twice as long again with half the pressure and so on. The result is actually almost unbearably wonderful for many women, so it's worth the discipline.

Man: After five minutes of thigh and leg massage it is time to move into more intimate massage. Stop massaging and make eye contact with your partner. Now ask your partner if you can start massaging a bit closer to Yoni.

Woman: If it's OK to proceed, give your full, conscious permission.

Man: If you've received a 'Yes', acknowledge it. Now resume your leg and thigh massage. This time, start gently, slowly and deliberately to move your hands towards your partner's Yoni at the end of each stroke. So, for example, if you are stroking on the inside of your partner's thigh, just lightly extend the stroke up the outside of her Yoni. In the beginning, make your strokes so light that she barely feels them. Then, on each subsequent stroke, apply just a little bit more pressure.

Continue moving your strokes more and more around the Yoni but not actually on or into it. Now slow your strokes down until your hands come to a rest on top of Yoni.

STAGE 5: MASSAGE OUTER AND INNER LIPS

Clear, honest and open communication about what is happening in a woman's body is a very effective way to open up channels for Sexual Qi to flow. However, it's not at all unusual for a woman to feel a bit strange about verbalizing so clearly what she feels and wants when it comes to sex. Aren't men just supposed to know what to do? Well, very often they don't, and when a woman trusts them enough to tell them, it's really sexy! Personally, I find there is nothing more attractive than a woman who knows what she wants and is not afraid to gently but clearly tell me. It gives me a lot more confidence that I'm doing the right thing. Remember that saying 'Yes' also greatly increases the chances that Sexual Qi will flow.

Man: Ask if it's OK to start massaging Yoni's outer lips.

Woman: Listen to the question but don't answer right away. Take a second to observe what is going on in your body. How do you feel? Relaxed? Tense? How does it feel to have your partner's hands on Yoni? Safe? Scary?

Sample Dialogue for the Receiver

'Yes, please. It feels really nice to have your hands on Yoni and I'm really looking forward to what's next.'

or:

'So far so good. I'm feeling a bit nervous, however, and notice there is still some tension in my legs. Could you do a bit more massage on my inner thighs?'

or even:

'Phew. I feel like that's all I can manage. Thank you for your loving attention, it was great. We can try more next time if that's OK.'

Take time to really notice how you feel and communicate this to your partner.

Man: If you've received a clear 'Yes', you can start with the 'Outer Lip Massage' (see drawing next page). First warm up some lubricant in your hand and apply it slowly to Yoni. Then, using your thumb and index finger, gently work your way up and down the outer lips of the Yoni. Some women enjoy it if you gently roll the outer lip between your fingers as you move up and down, while others enjoy long, slow strokes with just a little bit of pressure. Just as in the Sacred Touch massage, make sure you keep the communication and eye contact going until you've settled into a mutually agreeable stroke.

Take your time and spend at least five minutes on the outer lips. Then check with your partner if it's OK to start massaging Yoni's inner lips. If you receive a 'Yes', begin massaging Yoni's inner lips. You can use the same strokes as you used on the outer lips. Spend five minutes stroking and/or massaging the inner lips. The basic motion to use is upwards, i.e. from the Hui Yin up towards the clitoris. Although the stroke physically ends at the top of the lips, use your mind to visualize Sexual Qi flowing up her front channel to her heart.

Woman: The chances are quite good that you'll start to get some Sexual Qi and excitement flowing during the Outer and Inner Lip massages. Good! Wriggle your pelvis and breath deeply. Circulate your Qi. It's OK to make noises as well but if you do want to let out some sound, try relaxing your throat as much as you can. Deeper sounds can help open your channels.

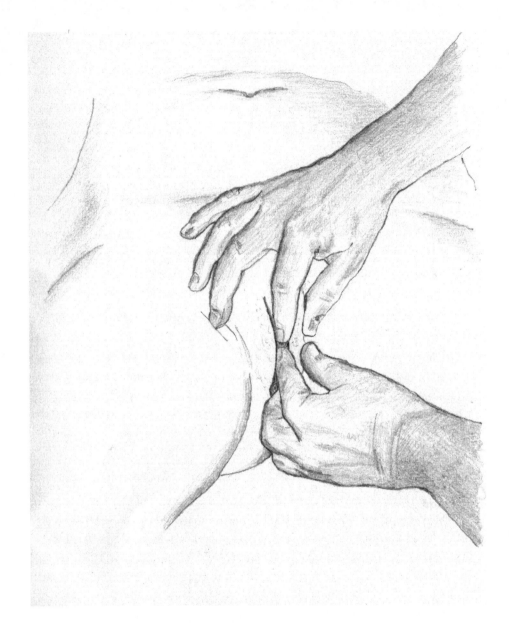

STAGE 6: MASSAGE AND TEASE THE CLITORIS

First, a word of caution to the man: please proceed with care. In many women the clitoris is very sensitive. This sensitivity can also vary depending on a wide variety of factors. A good rule of thumb is 'if she's not excited, it's probably not nice'. In fact, for some women a direct touch on the clitoris can be quite overwhelming and even painful.

So how do you tell when a woman is excited? The Taoists enumerated The Nine Essences, The Five Desires, The Five Signs and The Ten Movements as ways to see when a woman is aroused. Here are a few of the points they cover and which are easy to recognize:

- Red flushing on the chest and face
- Breathing becomes more shallow and rapid
- Yoni's lips begin to swell
- Yoni becomes more lubricated

So how do you bring forth Sexual Qi in your partner by massaging the clitoris if it's not by direct touch? Well, it's not an action/response situation, i.e. you don't simply 'do' something to her clitoris to get a response. The Sexual Qi will come all by itself given the right conditions. Sometimes those conditions are very gentle and sometimes they are more vigorous. Simply stay sensitive at all times to what your partner needs. This does take practice and time, however, so don't be discouraged if the results are not immediately earth-shattering. The important thing is not the goal but the journey.

The purpose of the Yoni Massage is not to bring forth a strong, explosive orgasmic energy. I suspect some people will find this a new idea, as for many people orgasmic overwhelm is what sex is supposed to be about. The techniques of Sacred Sex are designed to train you to allow more and more Sexual Qi to flow, without hindrance, through your entire being. You can then guide the Sexual Qi where you wish. It's not really possible to guide an explosion that's blasting through obstacles.

So, if an explosion is not what we're after, what is it? Whole-body orgasm with waves of pleasure moving through our entire being while breathing deeply and slowly accompanied by whole throat sounds is what. Work on staying conscious and present enough to 'breathe out' your orgasmic energy so it goes right down to your fingers and toes. This goes as much for the man as the woman during the exercise. The more you can synchronize your experience of the Sexual Qi, the better.

Both partners: If you are expecting or wanting something to happen, the chances are it won't. Most women cannot orgasm on command, just as most men cannot have an erection through sheer willpower. The trick is to relax and just enjoy being together and to accept that whatever happens, or doesn't happen, is perfectly OK. To do this in a world that is increasing goal-oriented can take a bit of 'un-learning' and patience however.

Man: Apply some lubricant that you've warmed up in your hand. Now, make sure you know where the clitoris is located. Don't be shy; if you're unsure, ask your partner to guide your index finger directly. Once you are confident as to the location of the clitoris, start by 'massaging around the clitoris'. You do this by making small circular motions with your index finger while pressing lightly next to the clitoris. Now, imagine that the clitoris is at the centre of a clock. Start with your finger at the six o'clock position and work your way slowly around 'the clock' in a total of eight steps all the while making small circular motions. At each step massage for at least ten seconds, all the time watching your partner for feedback.

Woman: Breathe slowly and deeply (you're getting used to this instruction by now, I suspect!). Try to still your mind by focusing on what you are feeling in your body. As your partner works around your clitoris, note when he does something that feels especially good. Agree a sign with your partner to communicate this as you may very well get to a point where talking is not going to be the best way to communicate. For instance, you could agree that if you raise two fingers it means 'Ooh, that feels good!' Most women find that they are particularly sensitive at certain points around the clitoris. This can be a great journey of discovery for you and your partner.

Man: Make a mental note of where the most sensitive spots were after completing a full circuit of the clitoris. Now check with your partner if it's OK to massage a bit more on the sensitive spots you've found.

She might enthusiastically say 'Yes', or she might need a breather for a second before continuing. She might not be clear yet on where her sensitive spots are, in which case you can simply do another circuit of the clock.

Spend up to ten minutes on the 'massage around the clitoris'.

Both partners: There's a pretty good chance that Sexual Qi will start to flow quite strongly now and this may even start to bring up orgasmic surges. If you feel these waves start to come, slow down. The man can also stop what he is doing and just hold his hands over Yoni and the woman's heart as the woman slows her breathing, relaxes her limbs and 'breathes into' her Yoni.

Man: Note that the clitoris can be a bit tricky to massage as it can 'come and go'. Just like your Jade Stalk, the clitoris can be larger or smaller depending on how excited a woman is. Sometimes the clitoris will seem to disappear completely as it retracts into the body. This happens when a woman gets very excited. If this happens, it's a sign to be extra attentive and slow down your movements.

Now check with your partner if it's OK to massage her clitoris directly. If your partner is getting quite excited, and she may well be, make sure that you have agreed on non-verbal 'Yes' and 'No' signals, such as raising a single finger or showing an open hand with the palm towards the man.

Move gently into the first step of the direct clitoral massage. Using your thumb and middle finger, gently squeeze and slide up and off the clitoris with a very slight pulling pressure. Watch your partner carefully as you do this, as her feedback will help you gauge the correct pressure and speed to use. Do this nine times and stop for a second. Then do another nine strokes and rest.

This 'nine strokes and rest' rhythm is very important. Sexual Qi can rise just as much during times of inactivity as during direct stimulation. It's also one of the most difficult things to judge correctly, as some women like longer periods of activity between gaps and some can only take three or six strokes before needing a break. This rhythm can also change over time as you both become more sensitive and can also be different just because things happen to be different that day! There are no hard and fast rules; it's all about sensitivity and communication.

Both partners: So how do you know if you're 'doing it correctly'? It's pretty easy, actually. Just watch for the tell-tale signs of excitement (quickened breathing, flushes etc.) and pause when you see that there is a sudden increase in Sexual Qi. After you pause, you may observe that you don't return to the same starting level of excitement but that instead you 'move up a notch' each time. This slow but steady increase in the level of Sexual Qi is the key to the whole exercise.

Man: What you're doing is slowly but surely increasing the amount of Sexual Qi flowing through the woman's body. During the pauses, you give the Sexual Qi a chance to spread throughout the entire body outwards from Yoni. You can assist this during the pauses by stroking gently but firmly up the body and down the arms or down the legs. You can also move into the 'honouring' position with one hand over Yoni and the other hand on her heart. It also helps if you watch your own breathing and Qi circulation when you sense the Sexual Qi starting to flow. Sit straight, breathe deeply from your belly and circulate your Qi. When you do this, you will notice that it helps your partner to stay present and in her body.

After some minutes of clitoris stroking, try this:

Place your thumb and middle finger at the base of clitoris. Squeeze very gently and use your index finger to very, very gently 'tickle' the clitoris. Do this by curling your index finger and pulling it upwards, just touching the very top of the clitoris as you do this.

Do this three, six or nine times and pause. At this point your partner may not be able to provide verbal feedback as her Sexual Qi may be flowing strongly. If so, it's up to you to hone your sensitivity finely so that you don't push her into an orgasmic explosion. Please resist the temptation to do this, although that may be easier said than done.

STAGE 7: MASSAGE G-SPOT AND DOUBLE STROKE

Women have many ways of generating Sexual Qi; clitoral, vaginal, g-spot and nipple manipulation are some of the many possibilities. There's no right or wrong way to generate Sexual Qi. What is useful to be aware of is the fact that different parts of the body generate different qualities of Sexual Chi, some more intense, some more gentle. It's also possible, with a bit of skill and sometimes ingenuity, to combine different points to wonderful effect.

Man: You've now come to the last stage of the Yoni Massage. You're now going to do a 'G-Spot' massage. Of course, it helps if you know what the G-Spot is and how to find it! The 'G-Spot' was first described by (and named after) a German obstetrician and gynaecologist called Ernst Grafenberg. He wrote in 1944 that the G-Spot is a 'zone of erogenous feeling' that is 'located along the sub-urethral surface of the anterior vaginal wall'. This is technically accurate, but here's a simpler way to find it:

First, ask your partner for permission to work on locating her G-Spot. This means that you will enter Yoni with your fingers.

Woman: Make sure that you're OK with this. Are you feeling relaxed? Trusting? Lubricated enough? Don't hesitate to communicate honestly and make sure you feel 100% comfortable with saying 'Yes'. It is completely OK to take a break or even decide that you've gone far enough for this session. The golden rule is that you decide what is happening. The Yoni Massage is a chance for you to allow intimacy on your terms.

Man: After you've heard a 'Yes', place both of your hands on Yoni for a few seconds. Wait until you feel the muscles around Yoni relax and for your partner's breathing to slow down. The more relaxed she is, the nicer it is for her.

Now gently draw the middle finger of your left hand up and into Yoni. If your partner is very relaxed and wet you may find that there is no resistance at all, but you may also discover that Yoni's opening is still closed a bit. If you feel any resistance, simply stop moving your finger and let it rest against the opening of Yoni. After a while, Yoni will relax and you can move in a bit more. You can also try withdrawing a bit and then moving in again or very slowly moving your finger in a circle. The goal is to have a completely relaxed Yoni that is 'welcoming' you in.

It's very hard to give exact instructions here as each woman, and couple, is different. You're working with a very intimate part of your partner's anatomy and she may, or may not, even know what sort of tension she has there. It's not at all uncommon for her to start crying or experiencing other strong emotions as she feels deep love and respect at such an intimate level. That's perfectly OK. Just keep breathing and stay with her.

Once you have made your way into Yoni to the depth of your second knuckle make sure your palm is facing upwards. Now slowly curl your finger until the tip of your finger touches the skin behind the pubic bone. Feel along the upper wall of Yoni here. You can tell when you've found the G-Spot because the skin is a bit rougher or dimpled there.

So, what if you can't find it? Don't worry. The whole area is very sensitive and all you need to do is communicate with your partner and she'll let you know where she is especially sensitive.

Woman: Relax. Breathe. Keep eye contact with your partner as he moves into your Yoni. When he starts to move inside you, focus your attention on the sensations that arise. Some women actually feel like they have to pee when the G-Spot is stimulated so be aware of this and let your partner know if he's found the right spot.

Man: Spend anywhere up to ten minutes gently massaging the G-Spot. Try circular, up and down and sideways motions, all the time watching for feedback. The G-Spot is normally not nearly as sensitive as the clitoris so you can be slightly firmer in your touch. Just as with the clitoral massage, stay very aware of your partner's Sexual Qi If you feel that she is coming near to the crest of a wave of energy, slow down or stop the movement of your finger. At the same time, you can spread the Sexual Qi up her body with your right hand.

After a while, you can move into the Double Stroke, which is a wonderful combined stimulation of the G-Spot and the clitoris.

You do this by using your right hand to stroke over Yoni starting from under the clitoris and moving upwards while at the same time stroking G-Spot with your left hand. You start with your hands together and facing each other and then draw them apart in a single, fluid motion. Use your intuition and sensitivity when doing this as some women will enjoy some strokes and a rest while other will want to just carry on without stopping.

Since you're reaching the end of the massage, you can continue until the Sexual Qi peaks and flows. When this happens, help your partner to circulate her Qi by moving into the 'Connecting the Circuit' position and follow her orbit with your mind.

Woman: You may become very orgasmic as your partner stimulates you and helps you to release your Sexual Qi. If orgasmic energy does start to wash over you, breath deeply, touch the tip of your tongue to the roof of your mouth and circulate your Qi. On your exhalations, open your throat wide and make noise!

Please note that if you have not had a lot of orgasmic energy in your life recently, you may find that not much happens other than a deep relaxation. That's fine, as that is a crucial step towards allowing your Sexual Qi to flow. Each

Yoni Massage will allow a little bit more energy to flow. Simply relax and know that it will all come exactly when it needs to and, most often, when you least expect it.

Man: Check with your partner to see if she wants to continue or whether she has had enough for this session. She'll know!

Both partners: At the end of the Yoni Massage, move into the 'Honouring' position and feel the Sexual Qi circulating through your bodies. Visualize it being stored in both of your Tan Tiens. The man might be quite surprised at how energized he feels afterwards, even though he was the one giving the massage. When you've both relaxed, you might want to lie down side-by-side and hug and cuddle a bit. A whispered 'Thank You' from the woman is a nice way to complete the Yoni Massage exchange as well.

Yoni Massage Quick Reference

Remember to ask for permission between each stage.
- Gather Diffused Qi (15 min)
- Honour Your Partner and Connect the Circuit (2 min)
- Leg and Thigh Massage (5 min)
- Approach Yoni and Ask Permission (2 min)
- Massage Outer and Inner Lips while Receiving Feedback (10 min)
- Massage and Tease the Clitoris (10–15 min)
- Massage G-Spot and Double Stroke (10+ min)

Chapter 10

Jade Stalk Massage

The understanding

> What the caterpillar calls the end,
> the rest of the world calls a butterfly
> —Lao Tzu

Men can learn to choose if and when to ejaculate, how to separate orgasm from ejaculation and how to direct Sexual Qi throughout their body. This learning often requires a willingness to change at a deep level. Women can help men learn these skills by providing sensitive, loving and knowledgeable support.

The Background

When a young man starts to explore sex with a young woman, he often finds that he is 'fumbling in the dark' with little knowledge of how to consciously use Sexual Qi. Since Sexual Qi in young men is usually very powerful (most reach their prime at the age of nineteen), it's not uncommon for a young man to ejaculate within minutes, or even seconds, of entering a woman. This means that the woman has not had much of a chance to warm up, so the entire experience is a bit one-sided. If men don't learn how to pace themselves, they may find that their sexual partners are not satisfied.

Many 'primitive' cultures had an excellent solution to this unsatisfactory scenario. They simply sent the young men off, before they got married, to older women who taught them how to satisfy a woman. In fact, one African culture even made it a requirement that a boy had to be able to demonstrate that he knew how to bring a woman to orgasm before he was allowed to marry. Just imagine what our society would look like if that requirement were still in place. Maybe those cultures weren't so 'primitive' after all! In stark contrast to this enlightened policy most modern 'developed' societies do not teach boys how to handle their Sexual Qi at all. Well, the good news is that it is never too late to learn. But what exactly is it that men can learn? Two things to start with:

Manage your ejaculations

The Taoists observed that men lose Qi through ejaculation. The fact that so many men just turn over and fall asleep after an ejaculation is certainly a pretty convincing proof of that observation! The Taoists also believed that excessive ejaculation, in the long-term, was bad for your health.

Whether excessive Qi-loss through ejaculation is good or bad for you is something that each man needs to figure out for himself through a process of experimentation and observation. Most couples would agree, however, that a man who can manage to 'last longer' is going to discover very soon that a woman with whom he is practising Dual Cultivation will be most delighted. Remember, we're not talking about going from thirty seconds to two minutes; we're talking about the ability to last for hours!

Separate your orgasms from your ejaculations

In the section of chapter three titled 'A Western Scientific Explanation for Sacred Sex', I mention Dr. Lilly's work on the different pleasure-parts of the brain. The fact that the portions of the brain that are responsible for orgasm and ejaculation are not one and the same was a well-known fact to Taoists and Tantrics. The implications of this are, of course, quite an eye-opener for many men. Imagine being able to have multiple orgasms and not ejaculate! The good news is that this is not only possible but, in fact, is not all that difficult to learn. It just needs a willingness to cast aside some old beliefs as well as some dedicated practice.

So, should a man ejaculate at all if he loses so much energy from it? This is, not surprisingly, one of the most hotly-discussed topics when it comes to the practice of Dual Cultivation. Some of the most detailed advice in the Taoist literature does suggest reducing ejaculation frequency during the winter and allowing it to increase in the summer when there is more energy available in our environment. There are also guidelines which state that the older a man gets, the less he should ejaculate. However, I recently read an article from a (living) Chinese Taoist adept who explained that semen retention is no longer as important as it was. His explanation was that our diet has improved so much in the last hundred years that we no longer need to be as worried about losing vital life-energy since we have access to all of the nutrition we need now. This does assume that people are eating a healthy diet, of course!

My own experience is that, if you delay your ejaculation and raise the energy level of your Sexual Qi by circulating your energy, when you do finally ejaculate, you feel much less depleted. At the end of the day, each man can experiment to discover exactly what works for him. The important thing is that it is very useful to be able to make conscious choices about when, or if, to ejaculate.

Mieke's Story

So now it was time for the Jade Stalk Massage! We had been focusing a lot of our attention on me in our sessions, but now it was time for Stephan to be on the receiving end.

I read the instructions for the Jade Stalk Massage carefully. I tried to memorize it, as I did not want to sit there with the book next to me. It would take the flow out of it. The first time I tried, the massage did not flow very well, partly because it was new for me and partly because Stephan reached out to touch my nipples and my clitoris. It distracted me and I couldn't give him my full attention, which was necessary to make a success out of this exercise to give Stephan the experience of receiving, of allowing the energy to rise, of relaxing into it and letting it rise again.

I suppose men are different, but I still wanted him to have the experience I had had in many sessions before. It did not work out very well this time, but I told myself, 'we're learning, and there is always another opportunity to try again!'.

So, one night I told Stephan: 'Tonight I'm in charge. You just make yourself comfortable. Lie here; you are not allowed to do anything! It seems to me that when you are busy 'doing' you can't be with yourself in full awareness'. The game was for me to give a Jade Stalk Massage and then test Stephan on his ability to refrain from ejaculating, but in a playful way. He does like a challenge once in a while so he said 'yes' to my idea and it turned out to be great fun.

The Jade Stalk Massage flowed much better this time. I reminded Stephan regularly to breath deeply, to relax his pelvis, to do his circulation, etc. I found I could work better when I wasn't being fondled; I could pay better attention to Stephan. It took my full awareness to feel when to stimulate and when to slow down a bit. The aim of the exercise was to stimulate close to the point of no return and to delay ejaculation. I stopped worrying about following the book and tried all the things that I knew have stimulated Stephan in the past. I needed to watch his reactions very carefully. One of the signs I could rely on was that his eyes would widen when the excitement got strong. After a while, I noticed that Stephan was becoming a bit stiff since he was working hard on keeping himself from touching me. I told him to move his arms and legs a bit to loosen up again. Of course, it was all right for Stephan to touch me without stimulating me. Touch was important to maintain the contact between us.

It turned out to be one of the wilder sessions. But, fascinatingly enough, Stephan experienced several orgasms and managed not to ejaculate until much later. I was really proud of him, and pleased with myself too.

Stephan's Story

As I mentioned in my story in the Circulate Sexual Qi chapter, ejaculation control was definitely on the agenda when Mieke and I started doing Dual Cultivation exercises. I honestly don't think I lasted more than about five minutes in the beginning, which was quite disappointing for both of us. Learning to draw Sexual Qi up the spine helped a great deal but I soon realized that there was more work to be done. So, as usual, I went back to the books. This time I read about the Neo-Tantric Jade Stalk Massage which, in theory, was an opportunity to learn how to manage the ejaculation impulse and also separate orgasm from ejaculation. I was sceptical. I mean, I thought ejaculation was orgasm! But it sounded like a brilliant concept and I figured it couldn't hurt to try it.

So Mieke went ahead and arranged an evening when we would give it a try. She set up our Sacred Space with nice music, a fire and some incense.

'OK,' she said. 'Now it's your turn.'

We started with a nice, relaxing back massage for me.

'Now it's time to turn over,' she said.

I did and reached out to touch her. I really like touching Mieke and I can get quite excited when I do.

'Uh-uh,' she said. 'Tonight I do the touching. You just lie down and relax.'

Whoops. This was something new. I was used to being able to do what I wanted, when I wanted and I wasn't at all used to this situation. It wasn't that I had any objections to the idea, it's just that it felt really strange.

Mieke started the Jade Stalk Massage. It was lovely and after a while I started to feel excited, especially when I got an erection. I reached out and touched her leg.

'Hold on,' she said. 'Relax. Keep breathing!'

Wow. I didn't even realize what I had done. I suddenly saw that during my whole life what had happened when I got excited was that I always 'did' something. I literally did not know how to simply relax and be excited.

'Wait a minute,' I said. 'If I just relax I'll probably lose my erection.'

'That's OK,' she answered. 'I don't mind at all.'

Well, that was something new as well. All of a sudden I realized that I had a deeply-held belief that once I had an erection, I had to keep it. I believed that otherwise the woman would feel like I had lost interest and that she would go away or not want to have sex anymore or something like that. My arms that refused to stay still demonstrated this clearly to me. I had a very enjoyable Jade Stalk Massage that evening and did my best to relax and keep breathing.

The next week we had one of our normal Sacred Sex sessions scheduled, which usually followed a pattern of Yoni Massage, Jade Stalk Massage and a lovemaking session that might also contain some experimentation with anything new we had read about lately. As we started to get ready, Mieke said:

'I'd like to do things differently this evening.'

'Really?' I replied. 'How?'

'Well, I noticed last week that it was really difficult for you to keep your hands to yourself when I was working on Jade Stalk. It seems like you always have to do something or you don't stay excited.'

'Hmmm. That's probably true,' I said.

'Well, let's do something very different tonight. Tonight you aren't allowed to do anything, and I mean *anything*, at all. I'm in total control and you just lie there and relax,' she said.

I can honestly say that that was one of the most memorable Sacred Sex sessions that I've ever had. It totally turned my view of myself upside down as I realized that I, too, could receive. I also realized that Mieke loves to give, which is something I had completely missed all those years when I was so busy 'doing'.

Jade Stalk Massage Exercise

Goals

- Learn to relax while receiving sexual stimulation
- Learn to control ejaculation and separate ejaculation from orgasm

Duration

One to two hours

What you'll need

Your Sacred Sex Space together with your oil, your music etc. Some clean towels. The man might want to take a shower beforehand in order to feel clean and relaxed.

DESCRIPTION

In the Jade Stalk Massage, the man is the Receiver and the woman is the Giver. This exercise, just like the Yoni Massage, has a long, detailed description. You may want to read all the way through the description for the Jade Stalk Massage first before beginning.

STAGE 1: DISPERSING THE QI

The Taoists observed that men's Sexual Qi is concentrated in their genital area. In plain language, this means that when men get excited their attention tends to be focused on their Jade Stalk. When a Jade Stalk receives stimulation, the Sexual Qi 'charge' builds quickly, reaches a peak and then the Sexual Qi leaves the body via the shortest route, i.e. ejaculation. Dual Cultivation teaches a man to spread Sexual Qi throughout his body. This slows down the build-up of the 'charge' or urge to ejaculate and means that the 'point of no return' is delayed.

So why would a man want to delay his ejaculation? The obvious answer is that a man can spend more time making love with his partner, which gives her a chance to get her Sexual Qi flowing. The less obvious answer is that men, too, can increase, refine and direct their Sexual Qi by using the stimulate / relax / stimulate / relax technique.

Stage 1 therefore concentrates on moving Sexual Qi away from the genital area and into the rest of the body.

Both partners: Start your session with the Greeting Ritual as described in the Yoni Massage.

Man: Lie down on your stomach and make yourself comfortable. Put a cushion under your head if you prefer. Relax. Breath slowly and deeply from your belly. Let your attention flow out of your head and into your body.

Woman: Take fifteen minutes or so to give your partner a 'Dispersing the Qi' warm-up massage. Start with the man lying on his stomach. Try this: imagine a heap of warm, white clay on top of your partner's sacrum (the bone at the base of his spine). Now, spread this imaginary clay in a thin layer over his entire body by using long strokes that start at the sacrum. Pull your hands down his legs, up his spine and down his arms always making sure you pull away from the sacrum. Visualize that the warmth from the clay is spread over his entire body.

When you're done with his back, slowly turn him over and repeat the same slow movements. Avoid touching his Jade Stalk or testicles while doing this, as you don't want his Sexual Qi to rise too quickly.

Man: During the 'Dispersing the Qi' massage, you may feel your body begins to sensitize and even tingle a bit. Breathe into any part of your body that starts to awaken in this way. 'Breathe into' means that you take a deep breath and, when you exhale, you direct your attention to a specific area of your body. This helps you to relax and open. You can also practise gently circulating your Qi if you feel that you are becoming at all aroused. Observe what happens when you do this.

STAGE 2: HONOUR YOUR PARTNER AND CONNECT THE CIRCUIT

Woman: Honour your partner and connect the circuit as described in the Yoni Massage.

STAGE 3: LEG, THIGH AND HUI YIN MASSAGE

Sexual Qi flows best through a relaxed body. It's quite common for men to tense up when their Sexual Qi starts to flow, even if they try hard not to. Other men don't actually have a strong Sexual Qi flow and this is more common than many people realize. Many scientists believe that this is yet another side-effect of the PCB-related[1] xeno-oestrogens in our environment. However, most sexologists agree that the greatest cause of impotence, *i.e.* the failure to get an erection,

---

[1] Polychlorinated Biphenyls. See www.epa.gov/opptintr/pcb/

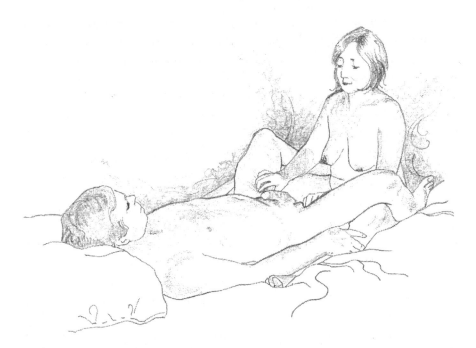

is tension. So you can't lose with this exercise as it helps create the right conditions for Sexual Qi to flow as well as dispersing it through the body.

Woman: Move into the Jade Stalk Massage position as illustrated. Start by using long 'Dispersing the Chi' strokes down the legs and thighs. You can then move into massaging or kneading the back of the thighs by reaching right up under your partner and working on his buttocks. Watch carefully for feedback about what works for him and adjust your strokes accordingly.

Man: Give positive, directional feedback. Stay very aware of your Sexual Qi and make sure to ask your partner to slow down or even stop her movements if you sense that you are becoming too excited. One of the great things about being a man is that there is a pretty obvious sign when this is happening.

Woman: As you feel your partner relaxing, focus your attention on massaging around and then on the Hui Yin point. The Hui Yin point (a point between his legs, half way between his Jade Stalk and his anus) is important for male health since massaging it also massages the prostate gland. Prostate cancer is the second most common killer of men over fifty and massaging the prostrate gland has been shown to have a beneficial effect. Start very gently and check with your partner as you proceed.

The first time you massage the Hui Yin point, you may find that the entire area is very tense and that you can't really get it to relax. Don't worry; after a while this will change and the whole area will start to soften up. This can take a few months, however, so don't give up.

Man: It can feel a bit strange the first few times when you get your Hui Yin point massaged. See if you can manage to bear with any discomfort you may experience while it's being loosened up. If it's very painful, you may wish to have your doctor have a look just to be on the safe side, but ninety-nine times out of hundred it relaxes and feels much better after a minute or two of massage. An added bonus is that, once you have relaxed this area, the squeezes that you do when you circulate your Qi can also massage your prostrate gland more efficiently.

STAGE 4: MASSAGE JADE STALK WITHOUT EJACULATION

It's not only women who have had negative sexual experiences that have left scars in their mind, emotions and body. Just think about how many boys have stories of being laughed at in the changing-room at school. Many men also have unhappy memories of not being able to 'perform' or of feeling sexually inadequate at some time or another in their lives. Other men ejaculate very quickly after being sexually stimulated and find this frustrating and upsetting. These bad experiences leave their marks in 'body memory' that leads to their Jade Stalks being less sensitive than they can be. It is possible to undo this negative conditioning and learn new skills, but it can take time. Just as with the Yoni massage, respect, love and awareness can make all the difference.

Woman: Make eye contact with your partner, all the while keeping your hands connected to his body. Now ask your partner to tell you about his Jade Stalk. What does he enjoy? Is there anything you should be aware of?

Some men talk about their Jade Stalk in the first person, *i.e.* 'I', while others refer to Jade Stalk in the third person, *i.e.* 'he'. I guess that's because sometimes Jade Stalk seems to have a mind of his own! As a woman, you can take the cue from your partner when it comes to how to address Jade Stalk. And men, if you're used to saying 'he', you might experiment with 'I' and see how it feels.

Sample Dialogue

'I'd like to know a bit more about you and your Jade Stalk. Can you tell me or show me where you are particularly sensitive?'

'What do you enjoy having done?'

'What can I be aware of that will help you stay relaxed while you get excited?'

Man: Now is *your* chance to take a risk. Go ahead, be honest and straightforward. Take a minute or two to tell your partner what you like. Vigorous and quick, or gentle and slow? Tell her where you are sensitive and what she should know. Do you like having your testicles massaged or are they very sensitive? The important thing here is to get the communication going so your partner doesn't have to guess what you like.

Woman: Listen carefully. Ask for clarification if there is something you're not sure about. When you feel you're ready to begin, ask your partner for permission to massage Jade Stalk.

Man: Make sure you can say 'Yes' wholeheartedly. You're saying 'Yes' to relaxing, being touched and, potentially, showing some softer sides of yourself.

Woman: Once you've received a clear 'Yes', begin working on Jade Stalk. Use some lubrication on Jade Stalk as it feels really nice. Continue massaging your partner's Hui Yin point with your left hand and start to very gently stroke his Jade Stalk with your right hand. You've now reached a very important stage in the Jade Stalk Massage where you are going to stimulate Sexual Qi with your right hand and keep the relaxation going with your left hand.

Man: Concentrate on relaxing and lowering your sacrum when your partner starts to stroke your Jade Stalk. Observe what is happening with your legs and thighs. Do they tense up when Jade Stalk begins to 'stand to attention'? Exhale and 'breathe into' any area that starts to tighten up. Watch what happens to the rest of your body as well. Do your arms and chest tense up? Relax them.

Woman: As Jade Stalk starts to rise, focus your attention on the other parts of your partner's body. Is he clenching his fists? Suggest gently that he relax his hands. Is he starting to take short, shallow breaths? Ask him to breathe deeply. Work together with him to maintain as much relaxation as possible.

Both partners: The idea here is to generate Sexual Qi in the man while creating as much 'space' as you can in his mind, body and emotions for the Sexual Qi to flow. Try to drop all pre-conceptions you may have as to what might or might not happen and try to stay fully in the present. It doesn't matter if an erection appears or an erection disappears. One of the things you may find out is that it can be just as exciting for the man to be massaged without an erection!

Woman: When you have got your partner's Sexual Qi flowing after some minutes of Jade Stalk / Hui Yin point massage, you can move into focusing all of your attention on Jade Stalk. Here are some things you might want to try, all the while watching and listening carefully for feedback:

- Gently massage his testicles, taking care not to squeeze too hard
- Use up and down strokes on Jade Stalk. Some men like a firm touch, others like a gentler stroke

- Do a 'twist and pull' stroke

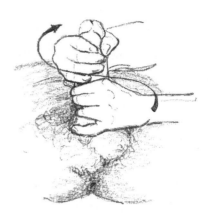

- Lightly stroke just the top of Jade Stalk
- Do an X-Stroke massage (see below) to the draw the energy out to the rest of his body

DESCRIPTION OF THE X-STROKE

Start with your left hand on your partner's right knee and your right hand on your partner's left knee. Your arms are not crossed.

Move your left hand slowly up the inside of your partner's right thigh towards his Jade Stalk. Gently brush over the testicles and Jade Stalk.

Continue moving your left hand over his belly towards his right nipple and out over his right shoulder. When your left hand crosses his belly, start moving your right hand. Move up the inside of his left thigh and over his Jade Stalk towards his left shoulder. As you move your right hand up his thigh, complete the left hand stroke over his right shoulder.

As each hand crosses either his left or right nipple, start a new stroke from the knee with the other hand. The idea is to create a continuous, flowing motion where there is always one hand in contact with and stroking his body.

Man: The Jade Stalk Massage is a chance for you to observe when the urge to ejaculate starts and to catch it before you've reached the point of no return. This takes practice. In fact this may well be something you want to practise alone if you find that the presence and touch of a naked woman is too stimulating. The technique is quite simple but you really do have to watch yourself closely. Stimulate yourself, or let someone else do it as in the Jade Stalk massage. When you notice that the urge to ejaculate is coming, stop. If you're working with a partner, you can say 'Stop' out loud or you might have an agreed-on signal such as putting your hand up in the air.

A good way to learn how to 'last longer' is for your partner to work on Jade Stalk for a given interval – 1, 2, 5 or 10 minutes depending on your arousal pattern. Then pause for a few minutes and circulate your Qi before starting again.

So what do you do when you feel the 'point of no return' approaching? The trick is to learn to relax so that the urge 'melts away'. You do this by exhaling into your sacrum and Hui Yin point and lowering your sacrum at the same time. This creates a feeling of space in your entire lower body, into which the Sexual Qi can move. On your next inhalation, you pull the Sexual Qi up your spine and circulate it.

Here's the sequence:

Man: You sense that the 'point of no return' is approaching. Give your partner a signal or say something like 'Stop' or 'Hold it!'

Woman: Immediately stop stimulating and move into the 'honouring' position with one hand over Jade Stalk and your partner's heart. Visualize Sexual Qi flowing through his circuit.

Man: Exhale through your mouth. Try to make a 'whoosh' sound when you do this. Relax your sacrum and visualize Sexual Qi dropping down from your Jade Stalk into the area at the base of your spine. Put your tongue on the roof of your mouth and inhale, drawing the Sexual Qi up your spine to the top of your head. On the next exhalation, visualize the Sexual Qi travelling down your front channel towards the Hui Yin point while gathering up more Sexual Qi from Jade Stalk.

Repeat the circuit nine or eighteen times. On the last circuit, pack the Qi in your Tan Tien.

Woman: Help your partner by visualizing the circuit with him when he asks you to stop stimulating him. You may find that it helps if you synchronize your breathing with his.

STAGE 5: RELAXING INTO ORGASMIC ENERGY

According to the Taoists, if a man ejaculates without having circulated and 'refined' his Sexual Qi, he is literally expelling life-force out of his body through his Jade Stalk. The Sexual Qi is then lost. Most men have no doubt experienced this sensation of loss but assumed that this is just how sex is, *i.e.* you get excited, ejaculate, roll over and fall asleep!

It doesn't have to be this way. But the difficult thing for many men is that the process of learning this is, to some extent, counter-intuitive. In the West, we're very used to using our willpower and focusing hard on achieving a desired goal. The Eastern way of approaching things is quite different. One of the things that I've found very helpful is attending a local Qi Gong / Tai Chi class. Recently the class moved to a new location in a sports hall where various other classes are held at the same time. It's fascinating to hear the other classes huffing and puffing and groaning while our class is practising to soft music with gentle, deep breathing. Yet I'm certain our Wu Shu Master has far more power and strength than the Western teachers of the other classes. I've seen him in action! In softness there can be great strength.

Learning to relax into orgasmic energy works in much the same way as Tai Chi does. What you do is relax your body while at the same time holding a clear intent and awareness while allowing your Sexual Qi to build. You don't push or force but instead stay aware of what is happening and use your mind to guide the Sexual Qi.

Woman: You need to be very sensitive and aware now. You are going to help your partner to discover a very special place – the space between orgasm and ejaculation. First, make sure you have an agreed 'Stop' signal, such as raising a hand in the air. Then continue stimulating Jade Stalk until you get the stop signal. You can help distribute any Sexual Qi that is accumulating by moving into the honouring position. There are other ways of helping to stop the ejaculation urge, such as squeezing the base or top of the penis, but I encourage you to help your partner discover how to relax into his body and distribute Sexual Qi rather than blocking its flow.

Man: As you are being stimulated, stay aware and watch carefully. At the very first sign of an impending ejaculation, give the 'Stop' signal. Pull your Sexual

Qi up your spine and then direct it down the front channel. When Sexual Qi reaches the bottom of your front channel, lower your sacrum and make as much 'space' as you can at the base of your spine for the Sexual Qi to settle into. Do at least three, and as many as nine, of these Orbits.

Watch your excitement level. If your urge to ejaculate has subsided, you can ask your partner to start again. If you still feel close to the 'point of no return', ask your partner to do some 'Distributing the Qi' massage to pull the Sexual Qi away from your Jade Stalk and out into the rest of your body.

Both partners: Have fun! The idea here is to take a journey of discovery together. Learn what works and what doesn't. If the man ejaculates, don't worry. Simply enjoy the orgasmic energy together. The more you work on it, the more you will learn about communicating with each other and becoming aware of the Sexual Qi flow. Sometimes the woman will know when the Sexual Qi is rising even before the man realizes it. Sometimes it's a surprise to both of you.

Man: When you do ejaculate, either inadvertently or on purpose, be sure to do some Small Orbits to circulate the Sexual Qi through your body and store it in your Tan Tien. It could take as little as a few days or it could take some months but the day will arrive when, much to your surprise, you orgasm without ejaculating.

Chapter 11

Daily Cultivation

The Understanding

All difficult things have their origin in that which
is easy, and great things in that which is small.
—Lao Tzu

Daily Dual Cultivation, when practised diligently with a committed partner and
with awareness, is a powerful method of permanently raising the level of Sexual
Qi in your body and between you and your partner.

The Background

The daily cultivation of Sexual Qi is called 'Morning and Evening Prayer' in
some Taoist works on Dual Cultivation. This means that you incorporate love-
making into your daily routine, just like eating, going to work and sleeping. This
is quite a new concept for many people as, for most couples, sex is something
that is done as a 'special' activity. Most people work on the premise that the right
combination of mood, time, place and emotion needs to be in place for a suc-
cessful love-making session. For some couples, sex is something they save up for
a special time, for others it has become an unsatisfactory routine for one or both
parties. But the idea that you would make love as a normal part of everyday life
is not something most people have considered.

The reasoning behind Morning and Evening Prayer is very simple. If Sexual Qi is a powerful healing energy, then it makes sense to generate it on a sustained basis rather than sporadically. One Taoist text I found states that the beneficial effect of orgasmic energy lasts in the body for up to fourteen hours. I'm not sure how exact this figure is, but most people have had the experience of feeling much better the day after a good love-making session. In fact, the good feeling can be so obvious that your co-workers or family tease you about it! So having a sustained flow of Sexual Qi through the body with regular twelve-hourly boosts makes lots of sense and is undoubtedly why the ancient Taoist health manuals prescribed regular intercourse as part of their healing regimes.

From a Western point of view, Morning and Evening Prayer also makes sense. For many people, the stress around 'will she? won't he?', 'should I', 'shouldn't I' etc. adds a level of stress to sex that is completely counterproductive to the production of Sexual Qi. Dual Cultivation is not based upon a lust-filled, super-charged sex blasting through any reservations we may have ('I couldn't help myself'). Rather, it's all about learning to generate Sexual Qi gently and lovingly, so the less stress involved the better. Setting aside regular time to practise Dual Cultivation without tension is a good way to re-train our minds, bodies and emotions so as to make the most of the Sexual Qi when it does flow.

Of course, for many people this daily practice sounds great in theory but is much easier said than done. Why? When I ask people this question, the most frequent answer I hear is that they have busy, full lives and couldn't possible set aside so much time. But how much time do they spend in front of the television? Is investing fifteen minutes when you wake up and before you go to sleep for something that can provide such a rich reward asking all that much? I was puzzled when I received this response until I realized that so many other factors come into play. A major issue is that, for most people, it's just not OK to say to each other, much less to their children or friends, 'we're going upstairs for our daily Sexual Qi generation practice. See you in half an hour!' Sex is just not something you plan, much less talk openly about.

The Taoist tradition has a much more matter of fact view of sex. It sees sex as one of life's fundamentals, along with eating and breathing. There is none of the moralistic judgement about something that, at the end of the day, is a basic requirement for the continuation of the human race. Although it took us a bit of effort to get started with Morning and Evening Prayer, we soon discovered that it actually feels very natural and normal to have a bit of 'cuddle' at the beginning and the end of the day. What we found through Morning and Evening Prayer is that there are many different ways of working with Sexual Qi, and they are not at all mutually exclusive. It really is OK just to spend a few minutes every day allowing some Sexual Qi to flow without it having to be a multi-orgasmic love-making session. The benefit of this becomes clear when you do have a fully-fledged session and you discover that there is much more Sexual Qi available as a result of your daily practice.

Mieke's Story

The whole area of sexual interactions with Stephan seemed to be covered with layers of tension and uneasy feelings. The excitement and pleasure had slowly disappeared over the years, almost without our noticing it. When Stephan suggested this idea of daily practice, I thought: 'Oh no; not every day, not twice a day!' He explained the idea, and that it was not like having sex twice a day, it was a meditation, a practice, like doing your stretches or yoga exercises in the morning. 'OK, I will give it a try.' I agreed eventually.

In the beginning, the practice was focused around bringing up some sexual energy and directing it to my womb for healing. We would synchronize our breathing, and together visualize the energy travelling to this area of my body. It took a bit of co-ordination, but it was not too hard to learn. There was not much sexual energy to gather up in the beginning. I was still very tired and run down, but I kept visualizing the ball of light that we created together, telling myself: 'Qi flows where the mind goes.'

At the same time we practised soft entry. I had been doing my solo practices: orbits, PC muscle exercises. I had done them when I was pregnant, but my pelvic floor muscles had become really weak. What had happened? I kept doing the squeezes whenever I thought of it, thinking: 'I can do better than this!' I used my finger to check it out. I had to admit, my squeezes were not very strong at first! Sigh! I knew that exercising the vaginal walls is important in strengthening the whole pelvic area. Now and again I asked Stephan: 'Do you feel this?' Hmm, he did not want to discourage me, but I could tell that he did not feel much really! 'Keep practising, and I'm sure I will start to feel it,' he tells me. Gradually the hard work seemed to be paying off. I felt we were becoming experts at this soft entry idea. This technique is not only useful for soft entry. I noticed that as my vaginal muscles became stronger, the squeezes added to my own pleasure as well: both during intercourse, but also during solo practice. I found that clitoral stimulation became much more pleasurable by adding some good strong squeezes. I also noticed that as my vaginal muscles became stronger, the upward orgasmic draw also became easier.

After some time of working on our daily cultivation practice, I noticed several things. The most important one for me was that it had taken the pressure off having sex with Stephan; we were learning new ways to be very intimate with each other. Somehow the layers of tension were slowly being peeled away. I could not have imagined that this daily practice would be so satisfying, that it would create a new bond between us. I felt it to be a special and precious gift we were giving each other. I really treasure this time in the morning and evening.

Stephan's Story

As I've mentioned before, my sexual education as a young man was a rather hit-and-miss affair. One of the unfortunate things I did learn (and I'm still not sure exactly where I got this from) is that, if you want to have sex with a woman, you have to trick her into it. Now I don't mean 'trick' as in fool or deceive. It was subtler than that. You had to buy her a meal and get her a bit tipsy, or impress her in some way or do something special, but the bottom line was that only when she got something she wanted would she consent to sex.

I realize now that this is a pretty depressing view of the whole man/woman sexual dance but the reality is that an awful lot of people play that game day in and day out. Personally, I hated it. But until I met Mieke, I'd never met a woman who just said 'Yes, I'd love to spend some intimate time with you.'

I met Mieke when I was nineteen, during a visit to a Buddhist community in the sand dunes of the West of Holland. I still remember, as if it was yesterday, standing in that caravan in the evening with Mieke and saying to her, 'So, where should I sleep?' I really had no idea where my bed was supposed to be as I had just arrived. We had just spent a few days travelling together with the community's founder and fallen in love during the trip.

Mieke looked at me and said, 'There's room in my sleeping bag.' I was totally speechless but I didn't pass up the invitation! That was twenty-seven years ago. But just because I had finally met a woman who didn't play games when it came to sex didn't mean that my 'baggage' that I had learned as a teenager suddenly disappeared. Since I still had the belief that women would only have sex if they got something, I never really trusted her in spite of her openness and honesty. In fact, it took a major crisis in our relationship fifteen years later for me to realize that these negative beliefs I had about women were slowly but surely poisoning our relationship. But even then I really didn't know how to change this negative view I held of women.

When we started the long, slow process of learning about Dual Cultivation some years later, one of the first things we started to do was 'Morning and Evening Prayer'. It seemed such a simple thing; you just spent a bit of time doing nine short and one long stroke without ejaculating morning and night. But something else happened, something incredible. After doing our 'Prayer' for a month or so, I woke up one morning and realized that something had changed inside me. Some deep anger or upset that I had had all my life when it came to women and sex was starting to dissolve. The fact that a woman was willingly, every single day, making time to exchange Sexual Qi with me was slowly but surely breaking down my long-held beliefs. A slow, gradual and gentle healing, but a very profound one!

Morning and Evening Prayer Exercise

Goals

- Learn the 'Soft Entry' method
- Learn two methods of generating Sexual Qi without ejaculation
- Learn to circulate Sexual Qi between yourself and your partner

Duration

Ten to fifteen minutes

What you'll need

Uninterrupted time and space

Description

Morning and Evening Prayer is simply a time you set aside to generate some Sexual Qi. One of the challenges we discovered right away was that erections are not always available when you need them! There is a solution to this called Soft Entry that you may want to learn. Soft Entry is simply a technique for pulling or sucking a non-erect Jade Stalk into Yoni. Soft Entry is also handy because it removes one of the major sources of tension for many men when it comes to sex, i.e. whether one can have an erection or not. Once entry is achieved, there are two types of exercise you can use – non-moving and moving.

Soft Entry Exercise

Both partners: We have discovered that the best position for Soft Entry is side-by-side (see illustration).

Man: Position yourself so that Jade Stalk is at the entrance to Yoni. Relax.

Woman: Take some lube and apply to both Jade Stalk and Yoni. Raise your top leg and use your hand to move the tip of Jade Stalk to the entrance of Yoni. Exhale and relax Yoni. Now inhale and 'suck' Jade Stalk into Yoni using the same pumping action that you use when doing the Small Orbit. You may have to practise a few times to get the hang of it but it's not difficult.

Man: Lie still and resist any urge to start moving once your partner has pulled Jade Stalk into Yoni. Just keep breathing slowly and deeply.

Woman: Once Jade Stalk is inside Yoni, continue the same rhythm of relax / pull / relax / pull. Make sure that you don't push when you exhale or you may well eject Jade Stalk! After you repeat the sequence four or five times, you can add a squeeze to the pull – first gently and then more strongly. You may find that Jade Stalk enjoys this very much and an erection will normally follow sooner or later.

Non-moving Morning and Evening Prayer Exercise

Both Partners: If you want to use Soft Entry, arrange yourself in the side-by-side position with lots of pillows so you can rest comfortably. The 'woman lying on top' position also works well for this exercise.

Woman: Touch the roof of your mouth with the tip of your tongue. On each inhalation, pull and squeeze Jade Stalk and then pull the Sexual Qi up to the top of your orbit.

Man: Touch the roof of your mouth with the tip of your tongue. Inhale at the same time as your partner and squeeze your PC muscle. If Jade Stalk is erect, it will move as a result of this. Pull your Sexual Qi to the top of your orbit.

Both partners: Exhale and allow your Sexual Qi to descend down your partner's front channel to his or her Hui Yin point and relax your PC muscle. Repeat the orbit nine times and then relax for ten seconds or so. Do three, six or nine sets of nine orbits, relaxing after each set.

Man: Note that the idea is not ejaculate during this exercise. Have an agreed on signal that you can use to stop the squeezing if you notice that the 'point of no return' is approaching. You may even have to pull Jade Stalk out of Yoni if too much Sexual Qi is generated. If you do ejaculate, try to do fewer orbits next time and slowly build up the number you can do without ejaculating.

Both Partners: At the end of the exercise, it can be a good idea to massage the man's Hui Yin point for a minute or so to disperse any accumulated Sexual Qi. It's also nice if the man holds his hand over Yoni to 'close the gate'.

Moving Morning Prayer and Evening Prayer Exercise

Both Partners: Start in either the 'side-by-side' or 'woman-on-top' position.

Man: Withdraw Jade Stalk almost completely out of Yoni. Move in until just the head of Jade Stalk is inside Yoni and then withdraw almost all the way out again. That is one 'short' stroke. Do this nine times at a rate of about one stroke a second. Keep your PC muscle relaxed during all nine strokes. Then, inhale and on the exhalation slide Jade Stalk all the way into Yoni. This is the 'long' stroke. Let Jade Stalk stay all the way in and inhale, squeeze your PC muscle and do a Small Orbit Sexual Qi circulation with your partner in the same way as in the non-moving exercise. Relax for ten seconds or so.

Woman: At the end of the long stroke inhale together with your partner, squeeze your PC muscle and do a Small Orbit with your partner.

Both partners: Repeat the set of 'nine short and long' three, six or nine times. Then change to the 'woman on top' position. This time it's the woman who does the 'nine short and one long' movement and the man stays still. We found that three series of nine times 'nine short and one long' in three different positions works well and takes about fifteen minutes to do. These instructions are not set in stone, i.e. be creative and find out what works for both of you. Ejaculation should be avoided just the same as in the non-moving exercise. Finish up with a Hui Yin point massage and a 'Yoni hold'.

Note: Even though you may use the same exercise (moving and/or non-moving) you will notice that, over time, your ability to generate and manage your Sexual Qi will change. The day will come when, quite unexpectedly, orgasmic energy will flow through your entire body when you are seemingly doing very little to call it forth. Simply enjoy it and gather up the Sexual Qi with your awareness and circulate it around and through both of you.

If you wish, you can consciously direct this orgasmic energy with your mind to any part of your (or your partner's) body that needs healing attention. Just as in the Small Orbit exercise, you simply visualize gathering your Sexual Qi into a ball of light and guide it with your mind to the relevant location and hold your awareness there for a few seconds. It's the world's tastiest medicine.

Chapter 12

Valley Orgasms

The Understanding

> A good traveller has no fixed plans,
> and is not intent on arriving.
> —Lao Tzu

Valley Orgasms are orgasms that take place when the body and mind are relaxed. They are one of the most effective ways to generate and direct Sexual Qi between partners. By not focusing on orgasmic climax as the intent of your love-making, you can pay more attention to the 'space in between' where Sexual Qi can flow of its own accord.

The Background

What is an orgasm? It's the peak of sexual arousal when all the muscles that were tightened during sexual arousal relax, causing a very pleasurable feeling that may involve the whole body.

—From a teen web site

I suspect that for many people the above quote is probably a fairly accurate description of what they experience when they reach a (or the) climax in a love-making session. In addition, most men have an ejaculation at the same time as their orgasm. In fact, many men think that orgasm and ejaculation are the same thing. This description of orgasm also matches up pretty well with the biologically hard-wired excite / stimulate / release cycle that ensures that a man can impregnate his partner. From a Dual Cultivation point of view, there are a number of problems with this hard-wired behaviour:

- The potent charge of Sexual Qi that is built up in a man during the excitement and stimulation phases is lost from his body by ejaculation, together with the healing energy it contains.
- Many couples find it difficult to synchronize the excitement and stimulation stages of lovemaking as men tend to excite more quickly than women. This often means that the man has an orgasm and the woman doesn't.
- The Sexual Qi generated by the orgasm flows through a body that is tense with excitement. As a result, the orgasm is often confined to the genital area (especially in men).
- The orgasm, especially for men, is most often a 'once per love-making session' event. This means that there is no opportunity to 'raise the vibration' or 'refine' the Sexual Qi (more about this below).

Here is a graphical representation of a 'normal' love-making session:

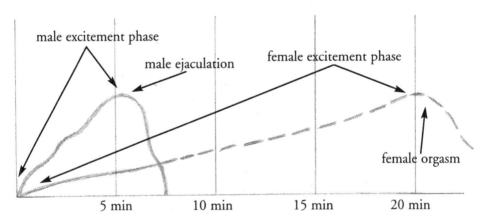

This graphs shows, in a snapshot, the all-too-familiar, hard-wired excitement cycle that so many couples have experienced. The man becomes excited quickly, lasts for one to maybe ten minutes, ejaculates and then rolls over and falls asleep. Most women, on the other hand, need between fifteen and twenty minutes to get excited, so just as they are getting warmed up he is falling asleep. You don't need to be a trained sexologist to realize that this is not a recipe for sexual relationship bliss!

The Taoist adepts discovered that if you modify this hard-wired behaviour you can:

- Retain the Sexual Qi in the body and use it for healing and energy gain. By doing this, the amount of Sexual Qi lost by the man is significantly reduced when he does finally ejaculate.

- Synchronize the man and the woman's excitement and stimulation phases so that both partners reach their orgasmic climax simultaneously.

- Experience whole-body orgasm by allowing the Sexual Qi to spread through a relaxed body.

- Enjoy multiple orgasms per love-making session by separating ejaculation and orgasm. This allows the couple to refine or raise the vibration of their Sexual Qi.

Here is a diagram of a Dual Cultivation love-making session:

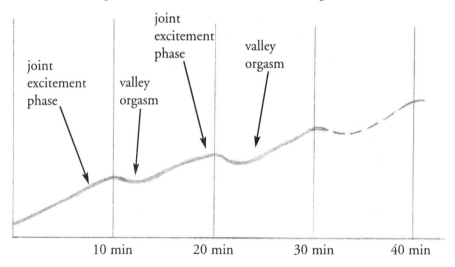

This couple made sure that the woman had a nice Yoni Massage first. This gave her a chance to get nicely warmed up so that, when her partner was ready to start making love, her excitement level matched his. As they practised some Nine Short and One Long strokes (more about this in the exercise), they felt their Sexual Qi level rising. When they sensed that they were about 80% of the way to the man's 'point of no return' they stopped their strokes and relaxed while circulating Qi between each other. After a few minutes they started again but from a much higher level of Sexual Qi than before. Some Taoist texts state that if they can repeat this process seven times, the couple will be enlightened. Personally, we can't verify the enlightenment aspect but what we can say is that an incredible amount of Sexual Qi is generated that can be used in very positive ways.

Is there any way to tell if you've managed to refine your Sexual Qi other than by how excited you get? What Mieke and I have both observed is that we can see the results the next day after a session where we both felt that the Sexual Qi was flowing well and where we consciously worked on Valley Orgasms. We've noticed that we are more alert, emotionally balanced and can even get more work done. This happens so regularly and with such consistency that we are confident that there is a clear cause and effect in operation. The fact that Mieke healed herself by directing refined Sexual Qi to her reproductive system is, for us, the real 'proof of the pudding'.

So that's it in a nutshell. Generate / relax / circulate / direct Sexual Qi and then repeat. Each cycle refines and increases the Sexual Qi as you make your way up the orgasmic energy spiral.

Mieke and Stephan's Story

For the first twenty years of our relationship we made love quite a lot (with four lovely children as the result!). We never talked much about our sex-life though, and we certainly never spoke while we were making love. Mieke felt that love-making was an 'inner experience' and that talking would be a distraction, and I thought that the whole point of the exercise was to get so excited that words would be superfluous. To top it off, we never did make much noise for fear of waking the children. So love-making tended to be a quiet affair.

When we started working on the Valley Orgasm technique we soon realized that we *had* to talk. Hand signals were just not going to do the trick when it came to the split-second timing needed to judge when to pull back from 'the point of no return'. I also found it worked much better to simply ask Mieke what was nice or what she wanted, just like I had learned to do during the Yoni massage. So, slowly but surely, we discovered that it was OK to talk during love-making and that it didn't 'break the spell' or 'spoil the mood'. What was most surprising, however, was that we found that just the opposite happened.

One evening, during one of our Valley Orgasm practice sessions, I had reached the point where I knew that I was going to have to have a break. After a few months of practice I was getting to recognise the tell-tale signs of 'excess Sexual Qi build-up'. Put quite simply, I would reach a point where any further stimulation, no matter how little, would lead to ejaculation. So I had learned that the best tactic at that point was to take a break and do something that did not involve Jade Stalk stimulation. So I stopped moving and let Jade Stalk rest in Yoni and then said to Mieke:

'I think it's time for a break.'

We both relaxed and circulated our Qi and let the Sexual Qi flow out into our bodies. It was lovely and relaxing. I then leaned back and looked at her and said:

'Would Yoni like a little kiss?'

At that she exploded into a tremendous orgasm which, not surprisingly, meant that I too ejaculated from the squeezes and the orgasmic energy. It was one of the most powerful orgasmic surges we had ever experienced. That was of course wonderful, although it wasn't quite what we had planned. What was most amazing, though, is that we realized at that moment that we hadn't actually done anything physical at all. All I did was say something! It seems like that space of relaxation can be very powerful indeed.

Valley Orgasm Exercise

Goals

- Learn how to create the right conditions for a Valley Orgasm
- Practice refining and directing Sexual Qi

What you'll need

Your Sacred Sex Space

Description

Both Partners: Before you begin, give each other a back massage and, if you wish, a short Yoni and/or Jade Stalk massage. The idea is to relax your bodies and to get a bit of Sexual Qi flowing.

When you're ready, move into a relaxed love-making position, *i.e.* one where you can stop moving and simply hold each other without having to tense any muscles. You also want to use a position where the man is not stimulated strongly. A 'woman-on-top' position can be a good one to try, but if you've been doing

Morning and Evening Prayer you will probably have discovered the best position for you as a couple.

In the beginning, the important thing to watch is the excitement level of the man. Start working your way up to a 'peak' of arousal using the nine short, one long stroke method. Once you feel that you have reached about three quarters of the way to the 'point-of-no-return' stop, relax and circulate your Sexual Qi up your spines and down your partner's front channel. If you are unsure when to stop you can use a small clock instead and stop after five minutes.

Now, go into the 'valley' by relaxing, synchronizing your breathing and not moving. If you want, you can hold each other but not too tightly as you want to leave room for the Sexual Qi to flow. This is the place where a Valley Orgasm happens. It may not happen the first time you do this, or even the tenth, but sooner or later it will. It can start as a small trembling or shaking that spreads its way from your bellies and works it ways all the way to the tips of your toes and fingers. It can also be an almost explosive energy that occurs when you least expect it. The important thing is that it happens 'by itself', *i.e.* when you are not actively moving and stimulating Jade Stalk, Yoni or any other part of your body. The wonderful thing about a Valley Orgasm is that you can relax into it and allow it to flood inside yourselves and between each other with full awareness.

This, then, is the point, in our experience, where the maximum healing

effect of Dual Cultivation can take place. As the surge of Orgasmic Energy / Sexual Qi flows through your body, take a deep breath together and 'gather up' the Sexual Qi with your mind. Exhale together and direct it to one of the following places:

- A place in your or your partner's body that requires healing or strengthening. Agree ahead of time where this place is so that you can focus together on it. This is how we healed Mieke.
- Your Lower Tan Tien for storage.
- It is also possible to direct the Sexual Qi to a particular 'thought' or 'wish'. This practice is well known in Western esoteric traditions as 'Sex Magick' and is outside the scope of this book. This practice should no doubt be undertaken with great caution and due consideration. There is a well-known Chinese curse: 'May all your wishes be granted'!

Once the wave of a Valley Orgasm has subsided, you can begin your nine short, one long rhythm again. Alternate roles, *i.e.* let the man do the strokes for one series of nine times nine and then let the woman do the next series. All the time stay aware and watch that your peaks don't get too high! Repeat the peak / valley sequence as many times as you like.

When you get to the point where you decide to 'go for it', just let the Sexual Qi reach a climax. When you do, remember to circulate and store your Sexual

Qi in your Lower Tan Tiens since, this is a precious, beneficial energy that you have worked on cultivating. Make the most of it.

Chapter 13

Sacred Sex Sessions

The Understanding and Background

Because higher and higher unions of Yin and Yang
are necessary for the conception of higher life, some students
may be instructed in the art of dual cultivation,
in which Yin and Yang are directly integrated in the art of
sexual intercourse. If genuine virtue and true mastery come
together the practice can bring about a profound balancing
of the student's gross and subtle energies.

—Lao Tzu

The idea of setting aside some time for sex is not totally foreign to most people but, unfortunately, it often happens that the plan is not agreed to by both parties. How many dates or evenings start out with one person thinking it would be great to have sex later on only to find that, when it comes to it, the other person is not at all interested? For many people, especially women, it's simply not acceptable or comfortable to agree ahead of time that sex is on the agenda. Often there needs to be an elaborate ritual first or, in a worst case scenario, alcohol or drugs are used to overcome inhibitions or to gain consent from an otherwise unwilling partner. Neither of these situations is conducive to Sacred Sex as they both involve blocks to open and clear communication.

The alternative to this 'hit and miss' approach to sex is for both partners to schedule a Sacred Sex session together. A Sacred Sex session is time (usually 2 to 4 hours although it could be a whole weekend) you reserve to work in a structured way with everything you have learned about trust, communication, touch and Sexual Qi generation and circulation. Agreeing a time and place for Sacred Sessions together is, in our experience, a very important step in saying 'Yes' and is just as important as practising daily with Morning and Evening Prayer. By doing this you acknowledge that Dual Cultivation is an important activity that needs, and is worthy of, a special place and time in both of your lives. In Eastern cultures there is a long tradition of Sacred Sessions and there were even temples dedicated to providing a place for this activity. It is one of the sadder aspects of Western culture that such a fundamental and wonderful activity has often been relegated to dark rooms with the lights out. Sacred Sex sessions are a wonderful antidote to this.

Stephan's Story

This business of having sex with a woman had, for me, always been a slightly stressful exercise. Does she really want to make love with me? Do I actually know what I'm doing? What does she want and do I know how to provide this, etc.? I know, I should just have learned to relax and enjoy myself but I'm a bit of a perfectionist and used to set ridiculously high standards for myself. Add this onto a slightly compulsive nature and you've got a recipe for disaster when it comes to having a good, relaxed love-making session.

When I first read about the idea of a Sacred Session I immediately saw the beauty of it. The idea of having some sort of a structure really appealed to me. I understood instantly that this would give me a chance to do a bit of preparation to hopefully ensure a good outcome. I really did work hard to get ready including doing some 'Tongue Kung-fu' exercises, locating and purchasing high-quality lube, ordering special Tantric music, etc.

The time for our first Session arrived and I set up all the bits and pieces, lit a fire and put on the music. We went through our plan, which was not very ambitious since this was our first session, after all. We started off just fine. Unfortunately, at one point I started to get excited and decided to jump ahead.

'Hold on,' Mieke said. 'That's not what we agreed to do.'

Whoops. All of a sudden I realized that something new had just happened. In all of our love-making until then I had pretty much led the way (even if I didn't always know what I was doing!). It's not that Mieke was passive but we had never had any sort of communication in place where she could say what she wanted, and I guess I'd never really asked either.

What we discovered was that having a plan for our Sacred Sex session created an opportunity for Mieke to have a clear input into what we were doing in each session *and* a chance to hold me accountable to it. It wasn't about making me wrong; it was about making sure that we were on an equal footing. As a result, the Sacred Sex sessions turned out be a real turning point in how we related to each other in other areas of our lives as well. We soon discovered that our relationship works much better when we both have input and accountability in our decision-making process. Surprise, surprise!

Mieke's Story

Sacred Sex sessions are very different from our daily cultivation practices. We make time for them once or twice a week. The kids know what we're up to, and the phone is off the hook!

These sessions are our own creations. Together we shape our space around the fire place, sort out music, incense and find nice oils for massage. In the beginning, we actually took time to plan the evening. We carefully followed the plan, to make sure we would not get carried away so that each one of us would receive the attention we deserved, in more or less equal proportions. Somehow this was really important for us. When we were young, and 'in love' it was easy to take the time for foreplay, but after all these years, this was not happening anymore. I had thoughts like: 'Let's get on with this business of sex, and get it over and done with' or 'Unfortunately, another item on my list of things to do.' In my mind, this way of thinking had slowly crept in because somewhere along the way we had started to take each other for granted. We each had expectations that we had not checked out for a while. I also felt I could not live up to Stephan's expectations.

When we followed the plan, there was no need to worry, or feel inadequate. Knowing the evening was planned helped me greatly to relax much more. First of all, the focus was not straightaway on excitement, sex or orgasm. We took plenty of time to be with each other, massage, breathe, and really go slowly. I found areas of tension in Stephan that he did not know he had, and vice versa. I loved giving my full attention to Stephan, and then totally enjoyed having his attention on me. I realized I needed to know that I was going to get this kind of attention and plenty of time to stop my mind from racing ahead, thinking of all the things that needed doing. Often I felt I was suspended in a bubble of love and relaxation that went very deep and where time had stopped. My great discovery was that out of this deep sense of space and timelessness came an arousal

I had not known before. It built up slowly, and almost exploded in ecstasy. This was a wonderful gift which made me feel very special again, and made me appreciate Stephan's efforts. I'm grateful to Stephan for his stubbornness and perseverance. It was well worth putting in the work for it!

Sacred Sex Session Exercise

Goal

Learn how to structure a Sacred Sex session

Duration

Two to four hours.

What you'll need

Uninterrupted time and your Sacred Sex space. Some nice bathrobes or wraps.

Description

PLAN YOUR TIME TOGETHER

This may sound counter-intuitive but, in our experience, Sacred Sex works better if you plan it. Most people don't plan their sexual activities; it just sort of happens. Although this can be great fun as you just 'go with the flow', it also leaves a lot of space for uncertainty, hesitancy and possible miscommunication which can put a real damper on proceedings. If you decide exactly what you are going to do it creates a lot more safety for both parties and actually makes it much easier to relax. Does this mean there is no room for spontaneity? Not at all. What we found worked well was to plan the first hour and then check in and see what we should do next. Sometimes things were flowing so much we just decided to have a good time and ignore any structures for the last part of our session; at other times we realized that we had had enough and just wanted to cuddle a bit in front of the fire, while most of the time we actually followed a plan for the whole evening. The important thing, especially in the beginning, was that we had the safety of knowing that there was a clear opportunity to re-evaluate how things were going and adjust if necessary.

Here's what a plan might look like:

- Greeting, blessing and a short meditation.
- Some dancing to favourite music to loosen up a bit.
- A back massage with special attention to any areas of tension that need working on.
- A Yoni massage for the woman.
- A Jade Stalk massage for the man.
- Valley orgasm work.
- Relaxation and bonding.
- Something to drink and a shower.

If you've never had a session before, it might make sense to discuss your plan before your actual date. This way you can both relax as you both know what you've agreed to do. You can also ensure in good time that you've got everything you'll need in terms of oil, candles and other bits and pieces.

CREATE YOUR SACRED SPACE

Make a date ahead of time. There is something special that happens when you know a few days before your session that you're going to have some time with your partner to work with your Sexual Qi. You might even try doing something like sending some flowers or leaving a little note or whisper in your beloved's ear 'I'm really looking forward to tomorrow!' This is especially nice to do if, as can happen, you've been together long enough that you might just be taking each other a bit for granted. This is a chance to get out of that rut and rekindle the excitement you felt in the beginning of your relationship. Even if you're not in a rut, it's still nice to be wanted and appreciated!

When the time comes, start by preparing your Sacred Sex space and yourselves. Many people feel fresher and more present after a shower or a bath and this can be a good way to allow yourself to make a clear distinction between your normal life activities and your Sacred Sex time. Ensure as much as possible that you won't be interrupted by telephones, children or any other distractions. Work together on creating your space so that you both 'own' it.

After your shower, or before you start, change into your light bathrobe or wrap and bless your space with the Greeting Ritual. If you want you can extend the ritual with a short meditation as described in the beginning of the Yoni Meditation.

REVIEW YOUR PLAN

Now go over your plan and make sure you're still both happy with what you've agreed to. We found that, in the first few sessions, it is really important to stick to your plan. Trust-building happens when you keep agreements and it is not at all helpful if, all of sudden, one or other of you starts to introduce elements that were not agreed in advance. This is especially important if you are trying new exercises; what may seem like 'no big thing' for the one partner may, for the other one, involve some serious stretching and risk-taking. Keeping to your plan is a good way to create safety for 'stretching and growing'. Remember, there are always (hopefully!) more sessions where you can bring in new activities.

MOVE THROUGH YOUR PLAN USING FEEDBACK POINTS

It might sound like a real mood-killer but we found that 'checking-in' with each other before each step of the plan works well. This is especially true when you get really excited and just want to let go and enjoy yourselves. It takes discipline and a will of steel sometimes, but we discovered that if you don't just hop over a step, you can build a delicious tension into your session. It's really nice and tough at the same time to know that something lovely is coming up, but that you have to wait and stay focused on what is happening now. This is a great chance to learn to pace yourself in an era of instant gratification!

The feedback is also very important as it gives both partners a 'safety valve'. This means that if things need adjusting, you both know that there is a natural point at which to communicate this. This can be something as simple as, 'please could I have a bit more massage on my left shoulder as I realize it's really stiff?'. It can also be something more complex like, 'that Yoni massage really brought up some old stuff around how I feel about myself. Could I have a bit of a cuddle and some reassurance for a few minutes?'.

It's OK to stop your session for any reason. Really. No reasons need be given; you can simply say, 'I think I've done enough for this session'. There is absolutely no way that either of you can know what might (or might not) happen with your inner energy as you raise and refine your Sexual Qi. It's completely normal for seemingly-unrelated things – such as a sudden cramp, unexpected emotions or complete loss of physical energy leading to sleep – to occur. Increasing the flow of Sexual Qi through the body can have profound healing effects and sometimes our mind, body and emotions just need time to process and deal with issues that may arise.

FINISHING OFF WITH APPRECIATION

No matter what happens, it's good to finish off your session with a gentle round of appreciation.

> ### Sample appreciations
>
> 'That was a great back-massage.'
>
> 'Did you notice how much Yoni loved that kiss of yours?'
>
> 'I love the way you seemed to know before I did that we needed to pull back so I wouldn't ejaculate.'
>
> 'That second-to-last orgasm actually made my toes curl!'

It's great to be appreciated and it helps keep the energy between you loving and caring.

BEFORE YOUR NEXT SESSION

When planning your next session, you might find it useful to gently review your previous one. This is where you get to listen to each other's suggestions and you can feel safe presenting them because you both know that it is perfectly OK to say, 'sounds great but I'm not sure that's my cup of tea!'.

Chapter 14

Variety is the Spice of Life

The Understanding

Life is a series of natural and spontaneous changes.
Don't resist them - that only creates sorrow.
Let reality be reality. Let things flow naturally
forward in whatever way they like.

—Lao Tzu

When the same pathway is repeatedly used for Sexual Qi, the amount of flow required to achieve the same effect increases. As a result, sensitivity can be dulled over time. Variety counteracts this and keeps the Sexual Qi flow alive and sparkling.

The Background

A common issue that often arises with couples in long-term relationships is 'sex is boring; we just do the same old thing'. There is a great deal of helpful advice available from many sources on how to 'spice things up' and, by all accounts, that is exactly what many people are trying. Twenty-five years ago, the idea that a woman would walk into a High Street shop and buy a vibrator would have been unthinkable for many people. Today, sales of the 'Rampant Rabbit vibrator' have gone through the roof and my daughters, when queried, tell me that 'oh, everyone's got one of those!' How does all of this fit into the practice of Sacred Sex, though? The Tantrics and Taoists didn't have sex toys, did they? Oh yes they did! In fact, historians and archaeologists have found a stunning array of dildos, aphrodisiacs, and illustrated sex guides from both cultures stretching back thousands of years. Just about the only things they didn't have were batteries!

So what is the purpose of all of this sexual variety? Simply to create ever-new and interesting ways of stimulating sexual energy? In part, yes. But there is another, deeper, reason behind the variety of sexual activities displayed. I recently read a very interesting article by a sexologist in response to the question 'can I become addicted to my vibrator?' Her answer, in short, was 'No, and yes.' On the one hand, there is no clinical proof that you can become addicted to any particular method of sexual stimulation. On the other hand, it is very clear that you can train your body to become used to one particular method of stimulation which, if repeated regularly, creates a 'groove' or 'channel' that your Sexual Qi learns to flow through. As the groove deepens, you need more and more Sexual Qi to fill it up in order to create the same sensation. This process can also be explained in a biological way. When Sexual Qi flows through our body, it produces dopamine in our brain. Repeated stimulation in the same fashion can lead to dopamine-tolerance. This means, in less scientific terms, that you need more and more stimulation to create the same degree of sensation.

The sexologist's advice was to put the vibrator away for a while and learn to use other methods to generate orgasmic energy in order to allow the body to 'unlearn'. In our experience, this 'groove creation' happens whether you use a vibrator or simply use the same position or love-making pattern over time. Sooner or later, your body needs more stimulation to create Sexual Qi if you use the same method all the time. Conversely, if you vary your practice and use different strokes, techniques and positions, your body never has a chance to get stuck into one groove or dopamine-production pathway. This means that you actually require less stimulation and that your Sexual Qi has a much greater chance to flow through your entire body. A final bonus is that being creative – whether it be art, music, gardening or sex – is one of the best ways to keep one's life energy alive and flowing. So variety is, indeed, good for you!

Stephan's Story

Many times over the years I had suggested to Mieke that we experiment with something new or different to try and re-invigorate our sex life. To be honest, the response I received was often less than enthusiastic. The basic message I thought I heard was, 'I'm not really interested in sex with you, so why should I try something different?' In addition, I thought I sensed an undertone of 'why can't you just be normal like everyone else and stick to natural practices?' This double negative response was enough to put anyone off and I soon gave up on the idea of injecting variety into our sex life, no matter how many books and articles I read suggesting it was the thing to do for a flagging relationship.

When Mieke and I finally started to talk about our feelings and attitudes to sex, I realized pretty quickly that I had not actually heard correctly and that my 'sense' was completely off. In reality, she just hadn't felt safe before and interpreted my experimentation suggestions as 'you're not good enough as you are'. If nothing else, this showed me, yet again, how useful those communications exercises were that I had resisted so much in the beginning. Once we had some basic safety based on trust and communication in place, I discovered that Mieke was actually quite amenable to discussing anything at all. That didn't mean she wanted to try everything we read about, but then neither did I. We soon discovered, however, that it was a lot of fun reading and learning about the incredible variety of human sexual experience out there. Some of it totally baffled me (I've never fancied being tied up and whipped, for example) but I began to see how different everyone is and that what generates Sexual Qi for one person is not necessarily what turns someone else on at all.

Since I tended to be the one who did the research in our Sacred Sex project, we soon settled into an 'I'll tell you about some crazy stuff I've just read about and you tell me what you think' pattern. What we discovered was that, when I first read about something new, we often found ourselves shaking our heads and saying, 'Hmmm. I don't think so.' But one or two things somehow seemed to stick or catch our attention and we would find ourselves discussing them again a few months later and sometimes trying them out. I also started to pay attention to things which I somehow sensed might be 'good' for me but that I was resisting – sort of like the process I went through when I first read about the communication exercises.

What I discovered after a while is that, for me, there seems to be two kinds of variety when it comes to Sexual Qi. The first type of variety is the thrill of the unknown or new. It can be really fun to try something you've never done before and it can definitely get the juices flowing! The second time can also be great but

I noticed that, by the third time, it's often not quite as much fun. Those particular practices often fall by the wayside after a while. The second kind of variety happens when we start to work with a new practice and I sense that a fundamental opening of a new channel for Sexual Qi is taking place. What seems to occur is that, once the initial buzz is over, I start to sense whether the Sexual Qi flow is increasing in a sustainable way or whether it's just a temporary jolt. It is like the difference between an adrenaline-based rush of muscle power versus strength built up over time. The sustainable flows are a good sign that this is a variety that is worth including in our regular Sacred Sex practice. Practising Sacred Sex outdoors (or at least in a tent) is an example of one such practice that we have both found to be highly beneficial.

Mieke's Story

I had always been very sceptical about having mechanical devices in my kitchen; I kept them to a minimum, wanting to do it the 'natural way'. I felt the same about vibrators. Why should I use a machine, when I have perfectly good fingers?

In the women's workshop, we were introduced to different 'toys': not just vibrators but other things, too. I had to overcome some resistance at first, but hey, we were all in it together, and I was not the only one who had not much experience with these 'playthings'! I learned a lot in a short time! It would have been nearly impossible for me to do all these things by myself; I'm so grateful for this opportunity.

One of the things I learned was to spend time with myself. I had never been very good at this but, after the course, I made a point of finding some time for myself. I found that it is actually important to make the time to relax first, to do something nice like listening to music, or take a bath, and only after this start 'playing' with toys or vibrators. I discovered a whole new range of feelings and sensations when using a vibrator. The vibrations actually relax the whole pelvic area and thigh muscles in a very different way, which cannot be achieved with fingers. I experimented with G-spot and clitoral stimulation, on their own and together, in different combinations.

I found it really easy to talk with women about these things; there was a feeling of us 'girls' sharing secrets, giggling, being totally honest, sometimes outrageous.... The women's workshop seemed just the thing that helped me to overcome another hurdle. It was not that I did not want to talk to Stephan about these things: it just felt awkward; I was not used to it. When I came back from the workshop, I felt inspired and full of energy, eager to try something different with Stephan, and we did! We watched videos, looked at the Kama Sutra for new postures, discussed different things we had seen. We laughed at some of the experiments we tried, and had a lot of fun together.

Things to try

This chapter is different. Instead of exercises, it contains a list of some things you and your partner might want to consider experimenting with. Talk to each other and trust your body. If it feels good for both of you, great! If not, try something else. Above all, relax and explore gently with lots of communication and at your own pace.

Massage

- Alternate light and firm touch. Use feathers, silk scarves, or your hair to provide lovely sensations.
- Lightly-scented (warm) oil is lovely.
- Feet are a very special part of the body when it comes to massage. There is a specific kind of foot massage, called reflexology, that maps the entire body onto the soles of the feet. You might want to get a little book about this and learn how to work on specific areas that need attention.
- Go on a weekend massage course or get a book/video on (erotic) massage.
- It's extremely beneficial for men (especially those over fifty) to receive an anal prostate massage. You might want to use latex gloves and lots of lubrication for this and proceed very gently and slowly with lots of communication!

Oral Sex

Fingers are great but tongues and lips are fantastic! Talk to each other and tell each other what you're comfortable giving and receiving orally. Find out what reservations you may have and see what you might do to allay any concerns.

Some oral sex pointers:

- Cleanliness is good. Perfumes and deodorants are not so good as they taste awful. If a woman or man is healthy, hot water and a little bit of soap is all that is necessary to be fresh and attractive.

- Oral sex can be very stimulating. From a Sacred Sex point of view, this means that you need to be very careful and sensitive and stop well in advance of 'the point of no return' for men. When giving oral sex to a woman, remember that many women have an extremely sensitive clitoris. Proceed with utmost caution and practise the start / stop / start / stop technique just like in the Yoni massage. In this case, less is truly more.

Helpers

There are a number of devices, also known as 'sex toys' in the West, that can be of great assistance when learning how to generate Sexual Qi. Almost all are for women. Here are some of the most common:

- The Jade Egg is a piece of stone shaped like an egg that has traditionally been used by Chinese women to strengthen and train their vaginal muscles. A piece of string is threaded through a small holed drilled through its centre for easy retrieval. There are also advanced egg exercises that involve lifting a weight suspended from the egg.

- Dildos have been around for hundreds of years and are very handy for g-spot massage. There are some special models, with a little hook-shape at the end, that can reach spots in a way that fingers can't.

- Vibrators allow many women to experience orgasmic energy (sometimes for the first time) when and where they want to. However, the stimulation they provide is concentrated on the clitoris and/or g-spot and, because it is so intense, the resulting Sexual Qi can be so strong that it can be difficult to stay aware and direct it through the body. Mieke's experience is that they are great but that you may want to take a regular break from using them, to avoid getting your body stuck in any particular Sexual Qi groove.

Different love-making positions

The ancient Indian book called the Kama Sutra, a copy of which may be a good investment, details dozens of positions, some of which are quite acrobatic. The different positions provide not only variety but also allow Jade Stalk and Yoni to meet at different angles and depths that stimulate Sexual Qi in different ways. The 'woman on top' positions are, for many women, much more fulfilling than the familiar 'man on top' or missionary positions. Another benefit of the 'woman on top' positions, especially for men who excite easily, is that most men find that they are more relaxed when they are on their back and can control their ejaculation more easily.

If you are brand-new to experimenting with different positions, you might even want to incorporate a 'try a new position exercise' into your Sacred Sex session. Dual Cultivation is all about Qi circulation and it makes perfect sense to try different positions and find out what works well for you. We also found that it's perfectly OK if a position does not work well for you or if you both collapse in a giggling heap while trying one of the more challenging Kama Sutra positions. At the end of the day, it's also about having fun!

Sacred Sex Outdoors

Both Tantric and Taoist literature mention the benefits of practising Sacred Sex outdoors. When you can generate Sexual Qi in direct contact with Nature, you will often find that the energy created is very powerful indeed. Unfortunately, it's not that easy these days to find a safe, appropriate place to do this but we've discovered that even being in a tent can be a wonderful experience.

You may want to consider a nudist campsite for a Sacred Sex holiday. We have been pleasantly surprised by the quiet, the respect and the cleanliness at all the sites we have visited in France and have heard good reports from other parts of the world as well. After a few minutes you don't even notice that no one is wearing clothes and, since there are all shapes and sizes there, it's a great chance to lose any self-consciousness you may have about your body. However, overt sexual activity is not acceptable in these sites so you need to practise in the privacy of your tent and/or caravan just as you would anywhere else. The nice thing is that you don't have to worry about getting undressed first.

Dual Cultivation and Variety

This is one topic in Sacred Sex that, for many people, is controversial and is therefore conveniently ignored by almost all of the modern Tantric and Taoist literature. This is not surprising since modern social conventions, both in the East and the West, view monogamous relationships as the ideal. The sanctions for breaking this convention range from little or none in, say, San Francisco or Paris to extremely severe in some conservative cultures. Yet, according to research by Relate (the UK-based marriage counselling service), 32 per cent of men and 24 per cent of women admit to having an affair. I suspect that there are very few married or committed couples that have not had to deal with some sort of external attraction over the years.

One of the things that struck me when studying the ancient Tantric and Taoist material was how little emphasis was placed on 'couples' and 'relationship'. In fact, just the opposite appears to be the case. There are many stories of emperors and princes, dakinis and adepts, all of whom had numerous partners and learned the skills of Sacred Sex through encounters with multiple trained and skilled practitioners. If nothing else, the carvings on the Kamakhya Temple in India leave the viewer in little doubt as to what went on there. But these stories and histories are about a different time and age and undoubtedly refer to the activities of a very small portion of the overall population.

So is Sacred Sex something that is practised only in a committed, monogamous, relationship? Can it involve multiple partners? If so, what does this look like? This book doesn't attempt to provide any answers to these questions, but what it *can* do is give you some food for thought and discussion based upon conclusions from our (and others') practical experiences. Here are some things we've discovered:

- If you're uptight or scared about acknowledging sexual attraction outside your relationship it often makes things worse. If you can accept that it happens and talk about it with your partner, not only does the attraction often disappear or mellow out, but the Sexual Qi in your relationship can increase as a result. Many people find that knowing that their partner is sexy and attractive to other people is actually a bit of a turn-on. However this requires trust, honesty and communication amongst all parties.

- It's quite normal to feel sexual energy with other people from time to time, especially when you work closely together with someone. If you can be open and honest about it, and at the same time agree clear boundaries with everyone concerned, there's a much better chance that the whole situation will turn out for the best. It is possible to be sexually attracted to someone and not have to jump into bed with them, of course. What is interesting, however, is to learn how to do this without having to repress or shut-down your energy. You just learn to channel it in a different direction.

- You can learn, and practise, Sacred Sex with people other than your partner. But, ideally, this means that the other person is also an adept and that there is a very high level of trust and awareness involved with all the parties concerned. In practice, however, most people find that it's very difficult to do this. Our society does not equip most of us with the emotional and intellectual frameworks needed to allow this sort of scenario to play out well in the long-term. There are people and organizations experimenting with this in various guises. 'Free love' in some subcultures (especially in the 1960s), Osho-inspired tantric workshops, poly-amorists and even 'Tantra Swingers Evenings' are all examples of this. Our experience, however, is that it requires a lot of work to find the level of integrity and discipline required to practise Sacred Sex within oneself and a partner. When you add other people into the equation it can be quite difficult indeed. You may wish to proceed with caution and, if it doesn't feel OK, stay away. Trust your gut instincts.

• Sacred Sex takes time and practise. It's not really something that you can do well during a one-night stand. On a very practical level, the amount of time and effort required seems to point to working with one person that you are, most likely, living with. Most people in the West are very busy working, studying, raising children or otherwise engaged in full lives. They simply don't have the time to spend hours and hours practising Sacred Sex every day. If they can create twenty or thirty minutes a day plus an evening or two a week for Sacred Sex practice, then they've made a major investment. To do this on a long-term basis with more than one person is just not feasible for most people.

Chapter 15
Related Taoist Arts

The understanding

> The journey of a thousand leagues
> begins from beneath your feet.
> —Lao Tzu

The practice of Dual Cultivation can be supported and enhanced by using skills and knowledge from other Taoist disciplines.

The Background

The Taoist Art of Dual Cultivation, *i.e.* using Sexual Qi for health and longevity, does not exist in a vacuum. Traditionally, no one would have used Dual Cultivation techniques without having first learned inner alchemy meditation, Qi-circulation techniques, proper diet, Tai Chi, etc. Dual Cultivation, therefore, was merely one of many facets of Taoist knowledge. The complete compendium of Taoist knowledge fills literally thousands of volumes and would take many lifetimes to explore. It's only recently, however, that this treasure trove of knowledge has become more widely known in the West. Personally, I think it's fascinating to watch the meeting of East and West that is taking place and I have no doubt that both sides are benefiting in the process. The process of researching, translating and presenting this Taoist lore has definitely brought a new level of clarity to the existing Chinese source material. There are also many areas, such as Herbal Medicine and Acupuncture, where rigorous scientific investigation is casting new light on old knowledge.

What I have done in this book is present Dual Cultivation together with the other elements of Taoist energy-work that Mieke and I have used in our healing process. During this period we explored other Taoist disciplines and found many things that have enhanced our Dual Cultivation. The following is a selection of these. Have a read and see if anything sounds interesting. You may find, as we did, that other Taoist arts are waiting for you to explore them.

The Taoist Arts

Tai Chi and Qi Gong

Tai Chi (also known as Tai Chi Chuan) is probably the most widely known Taoist Internal Martial Art in the West. In general, Taoist physical development systems, including the martial arts, are quite different from Western exercise and fitness regimes. Ever since the Greeks invented the Olympics, much of the emphasis on physical exercise in Western culture has been on competition, i.e. faster, stronger, further. At a very basic level, you need only look at the muscled ideal of the male body that pervades the Western media to see how powerful this view of physical exercise is. In the East, exercise was, and is, closely tied to health and longevity. The Internal Martial Arts, such as Tai Chi, are particularly accessible as they focus on slow, gentle and relaxing movements that build up strength, agility and mental / emotional focus over time.

Qi Gong ('energy work') is actually part of the Taoist Art of Inner Alchemy (see below) but is often taught in conjunction with Tai Chi. Qi Gong focuses on generating and guiding Qi through a series of slow, meditative movements that focus on breath, stretching and concentration. In Tai Chi you move through a series of set forms that again allow Qi to flow through your body. I once heard the difference between Qi Gong and Tai Chi described as 'inner versus outer'. In Qi Gong, you concentrate on Qi and your body then adapts itself to the flow. In Tai Chi, you concentrate on the form and the body and as a result Qi flows. You'll probably find as many descriptions as there are practitioners but the end result is the same: more Qi flow and a fitter mind and body. Although it may be possible to learn Qi Gong and Tai Chi from books or videos, most people will find it easier to learn by attending a course given by a skilled practitioner.

The most commonly taught version of Tai Chi is the 'Yang Style Simplified Twenty-Four Movement Form' and it might make sense to start with this since courses that teach it are widely available. Once you have learned the basics, you can continue on your own although there is something to be said for practising and learning with others. It generally takes three to four months to learn the basic set of twenty-four forms. It's interesting to note that most Tai Chi Masters agree that five minutes of Qi Gong or Tai Chi a day is better for you than two hours once a week. The parallels with Dual Cultivation are clear.

Diet (Chang Ming)

Taoist Diet principles are simple and are based on 'living in harmony with nature'. Many people practising Dual Cultivation and Qi-circulation techniques soon discover that they naturally start to eat in a more balanced fashion and pay greater regard to what they put into their bodies. Here are some of the guidelines from the 'Chang Ming Diet Principles' that you may find useful:

- Eat until your stomach is no more than two-thirds full. This gives your digestive system a chance to process your meals without being overloaded.
- Avoid eating after 7 o'clock in the evening as the body naturally slows down before going to sleep.
- Foods to eat more of: local, organic vegetables and fruit, herbs, whole rice and whole grains.
- Foods to eat less of: meat, fish, salt, strong spices, artificial colours and preservatives and heavily-processed foods.

Herbal Medicine

The use of plants for medicinal purposes has been well-documented by the Chinese for thousand of years. Western science is now realizing that there is a wealth of knowledge available from this tradition. An example of this is a new, recently-released, low-cost treatment for malaria using Oriental Wormwood (Yin Chen / *Artemisia capillaris*) combined with a Western drug. Yin Chen has been used by Traditional Chinese Medicine (TCM) for centuries to control fevers.

In TCM, healing herbs are grouped into three categories: inferior, middle and superior. Inferior herbs are used to treat specific ailments. Some inferior herbs are very powerful and can, if used incorrectly, have serious side-effects. Middle category herbs are often used in conjunction with inferior herbs to distribute and assist their healing function. Middle herbs are also used on their own to strengthen bodily functions. You probably will only want to use inferior or middle herbs if you have a particular ailment that needs treating and only under qualified medical supervision. The only exception to this are some 'patent remedies' which are pre-packaged formulas that are normally sold either as powders (san) or pills (wan). An example of such a formula is Free & Easy Wanderer Plus (Jia Wei Xiao Yao Wan). This can be used as an 'alternative aspirin' and can also be very helpful when you are suffering from digestive system disturbances. These patent remedies are readily available at any Chinese pharmacy.

Superior herbs are potentially the most interesting from a Dual Cultivation point of view. Also known as Tonic Herbs, these herbs promote everyday good health and are traditionally used to enhance Qi, to regulate bodily and psychic functioning and as an aid to spiritual development. They are often taken in combinations known as Tonics. Interestingly enough, quite a few of these herbs are reputed to have aphrodisiac qualities. One of the most powerful is Yin Yang Huo (*Epimedium sagittatum* or Horny Goat Weed). This herb has been used for over two thousand years to replace sexual fire, boost erectile function and alleviate menopausal discomfort.

The study and use of Chinese tonic herbs is a vast subject and I've put some pointers to further sources of information in the reference section. However, I have done a great deal of personal, practical research over the last seven years and can attest to the power and efficacy of tonic herbs.

Acupuncture / Acupressure

TCM views body, mind and spirit as an integrated whole and believes that the origins of disease often lie in an imbalance of Yin and Yang in the body. The ancient Chinese healing art of acupuncture attempts to adjust the Yin / Yang balance of the body and re-create harmony by influencing the flow of Qi. Acupuncturists use very fine steel needles, inserted into a selection of three-hundred-and-sixty-one points along twelve 'primary' Yin and Yang meridians and two of the eight 'extraordinary' Qi vessels. Moxibustion is a related technique that uses small burning cones of mugwort to heat acupuncture points. Acupressure is the practice of stimulating these points manually through massage.

Acupuncture treatment would normally be preceded by a diagnostic procedure, called Zang Fu, that uses pulse-checking, tongue examination and a thorough patient interview. A Zang Fu diagnosis can provide the basis for the prescription of herbal remedies as well as acupuncture. The training period for a TCM doctor is usually five years, so it is not advisable to try either acupuncture or 'inferior' herbs on a self-diagnostic basis.

Acupressure, on the other hand, is a safe and useful tool that anyone can learn. In Dual Cultivation, the Hui Yin point (the perineum) is used extensively to relax and assist in the flow of Sexual Qi, especially in men. There are other points that can be useful as well. The Lao Gong points on the hands and the Yong Quan points on the soles of the feet are excellent points to massage to open up and assist Qi flow. Try massaging these points as part of a warm-up massage. You might also want to experiment with a smouldering Moxa stick held a centimetre or two away from the body as a wonderful relaxing tool, especially around the Lower Tan Tien.

Inner Alchemy (Nei Dan)

Taoist Inner Alchemy is based on an understanding that all the elements of immortality are found within the body and that the body is a microcosmic reflection of the universe or macrocosm. In Inner Alchemy, much attention is paid to learning how to direct Qi through the eight 'extraordinary' Qi vessels. The Small Orbit, for instance, directs Qi through two of these vessels – the Governing Vessel and the Conception Vessel. Inner Alchemy also contains the teachings of Dual Cultivation, where two loving individuals cultivate and direct Sexual Qi. When you study Inner Alchemy, you learn to use meditative (Nei Gong) and energy (Qi Gong) exercises to lengthen your lifespan and create an immortal 'spirit body' that transcends the physical world and reunites with the Tao. Even if the creation of a 'spirit body' is not your primary goal in this life (and by all accounts this takes at least sixty years of dedicated work), the meditation and energy techniques of Inner Alchemy can help you create balance, centeredness, peace and a sense purpose in your life.

Beyond Tantra Live!

BeyondTantra.org is an online resource created by Mieke and Stephan for people interested in further explorations of Taoist Sacred Sexuality. *BeyondTantra.org* is a members only site open to all readers of this book. All you need to do to gain access is fill in a simple form at:

http://www.beyondtantra.org/join.html

For a free one year subscription use the code **yintaoyang** when prompted.

BeyondTantra.org contains:

- additional articles by Mieke and Stephan
- forums where members can share their experiences of Sacred Sex
- links to other relevant sites including course centres
- links to online shops for Toys and Music etc.
- and more…

We hope to we see you there.

Mieke and Stephan

Reference

The following list of courses, books and music is a guide to what we have found useful and informative during our research and learning. We provide this for your information only, in the hope that it will be of use in any further explorations you may wish to undertake.

A larger and constantly updated reference section is always available at our internet web site http://www.beyondtantra.org. The web site also contains direct links to books, courses, music and other items and sites of interest.

Courses in Dual Cultivation

The following centres have courses in Healing Love. However, you would normally be expected to have completed some introductory courses before taking courses that work with Dual Cultivation (Healing Love) or to take a course that combines Tao Basics with Healing Love. Note that some of the Healing Love courses teach Solo Cultivation, *i.e.* work without a partner, instead of Dual Cultivation.

Universal Tao Center

Chiang Mai, Thailand   http://www.universal-tao.com/
Courses given by Mantak Chia and staff.

Healing Tao USA

http://www.healingtaousa.com/
Courses given by Michael Winn and staff.

Books and Videos

These are listed in order of how relevant and useful we found them to be when learning about Dual Cultivation, Sacred Sex and Taoism, rather than alphabetically.

Dual Cultivation

Chia, Mantak, *Healing Love Through the Tao: Cultivating Female Sexual Energy*, Healing Tao Books, 1991

Chia, Mantak & Winn, Michael, *Taoist Secrets of Love: Cultivating Male Sexual Energy*, Healing Tao Books; Aurora Press, 1984

Chia, Mantak, *The Multi-Orgasmic Couple: Sexual Secrets Every Couple Should Know*, HarperSanFrancisco, 2002

Chu, Valentin, *The Yin-Yang Butterfly: Ancient Chinese Sexual Secrets for Western Lovers*, Jeremy P. Tarcher, 1994

Yudelove, Eric, *Taoist Yoga and Sexual Energy: Internal Alchemy and Chi Kung*, Llewellyn Publications, 2000

Wile, Douglas, *Art of the Bedchamber: The Chinese Sexual Yoga Classics Including Women's Solo Meditation Texts*, State University of New York Press, 1992

Winn, Michael, *Sexual Vitality Chi Kung (DVD)*, Healing Tao USA available from www.healingtaousa.com

Sacred Sex

Anand, Margo, *The Art of Sexual Ecstasy: The Path of Sacred Sexuality for Western Lovers*, Jeremy P. Tarcher; Reprint edition, 1991

DVD – *Ancient Secrets of Sexual Ecstasy*. From http://www.tantra.com

VHS – *Multi Orgasmic Response Training for Men & Women*. From http://www.tantra.com

Ramsdale, David, *Sexual Energy Ecstasy : A Practical Guide To Lovemaking Secrets Of The East And West*, Bantam, 1993

Kenyon, Tom, *The Magdalen Manuscript: The Alchemies of Horus & The Sex Magic of Isis*, Orb, 2002

Taoist Healing and Philosophy

Lao Tzu, Brian Walker(trans.), *The Tao Te Ching of Lao Tzu*, St. Martin's Griffin, 1996

Lao Tzu, Brian Walker(trans.), Hua Hu Ching: *The Unknown Teachings of Lao Tzu*, HarperSanFrancisco, 1992

Reid, Daniel, *Complete Book of Chinese Health & Healing*, Shambhala, 1994

Kaptchuk, Ted, *The Web That Has No Weaver: Understanding Chinese Medicine*, McGraw-Hill, 2000

Reid, Daniel, *The Tao of Health, Sex & Longevity*, Simon & Schuster, 1989

Chia, Mantak, *Awaken Healing Light of the Tao*, Healing Tao Books, 1993

Kohn, Livia, *Taoist Meditation and Longevity Techniques*, Univ. of Michigan, 1989

Ming-Dao, Deng, *Chronicles of Tao: The Secret Life of a Taoist Master*, HarperSanFrancisco, 1993

Music for Sacred Sex Sessions

A selection of gentle, non-intrusive instrumental music.
Anugama, *Shamanic Dream*, Open Sky Music
Anugama, *Tantra*, Open Sky Music
Deuter – all CDs – New Earth Records
Karunesh, *Secrets of Life*, Real Music
Kitaro – all CDs – Domo Records

Kokin Gumi, *Zen Garden*, Avalon
Patricia Spero, *Silk and Bamboo*, New World Music
Rasa, *Devotion*, Hearts of Space
Robin Silver, *Full Moon* Hollow Bone
Solace, *Ahsaha*, Magnatune
Sur Suhda, *Images of Nepal*, Domo Records

Sacred Sex Essentials and Extras

Incense and Candles

Many people find that burning a cleansing incense such as sandalwood, Tibetan healing incense or white sage is a powerful way to change the atmosphere of a room. We have also found that for 'cleaning' a house or room Gum Benjamin is very useful. This comes as a powder or small chunks that need to be ground. You then put a small amount of the powder on a charcoal tablet.

We like placing one candle or tea light at each corner of our sacred space. Just make sure to place any incense or candles in a safe place where they won't get knocked over inadvertently!

Essential Oils

We use an essential oil warmer which releases the oil into the air. Here are a few scents we like:

Relaxing:	Lavender, Rose
Aphrodisiac:	Ylang Ylang
Invigorating:	Geranium

Cloth and Cushions

A special bedspread that you use solely for sacred sex sessions is not only practical (easy to wash!) but can also help to create a special sense of 'place'. A stack of towels is also handy for removing oil and drying off. You can also place a few of the towels under your bedspread. Finally, a pile of cushions in various shapes and sizes and of various materials with washable covers is a great way to make yourselves comfortable.

Massage Oil

Try to get some good quality massage oil. We have found Weleda arnica massage oil very good for stiff shoulders or joints, and the smell is very refreshing. Generally, however, we use plain almond oil, jojoba or grapeseed oil.

During sessions, we put some oil into a little clay bowl that has a stable base. You can also put some oil in a plastic squeeze bottle. We put in enough oil for a session and add a few drops of essential oil. In this way you always have a fresh pot of oil.

Lubrication

We have found that a good, water-based lubricant has made a huge difference to our lovemaking. It gives a luxurious feeling of smoothness and completely does away with any issues of being to dry for comfort. We have tried many, many different makes and have come to the conclusion that nothing beats the water-based lubricant called Liquid Silk. The great thing about Liquid Silk is that it doesn't get sticky and you can just add a bit of water as your session progresses to 'refresh' it.

If you use condoms, make sure you use a water-based lubricant as oil-based lubes can damage latex.

Other bit and pieces

•   If possible, a completely separate mattress that you use only for your sacred sex sessions. Ideally it would be great to have your own temple but most houses don't have this facility (yet!).

•   Easy access to a shower.

•   A jug of fresh drinking water and a couple of glasses.

•   A box of tissues and/or baby wipes.

•   Music (see separate list). An mp3 player such as an iPod connected to a stereo or speaker can be really handy since you can create a playlist with hours of music without having to get up to change CDs.

Glossary

Acupuncture (Latin: *acus* 'needle' and *pungere* 'prick') The TCM therapeutic practice of inserting needles into 'acupuncture points' located along the Meridians to release, unblock and re-balance Qi in the body.

Dakini (Sanskrit: 'sky dancer') Indian Tantric priestess. Also known as angels.

Dual Cultivation Taoist practices for couples that use the energy generated by sexual activity for physical, mental and spiritual self-development.

Feng Shui (Chinese: 'wind and water') Taoist practice of placing and arranging building and objects to be in harmony with nature.

Hui Yin Point An acupuncture point (CV1) located halfway between the genitals and the anus; called the perineum in the West. The Hui Yin Point is where the front (Conception Vessel) and rear (Governor Vessel) Qi meridians of the body intersect.

Jade Stalk The male sexual organ.

Kama Sutra An ancient Indian text on sex, most likely written between the first and sixth centuries A.D.

Kegel Exercises Named after Dr Arnold Kegel. They are designed to exercise the pubococcygeal or 'PC' muscles. Also known as pelvic floor exercises.

Kundalini (Sanskrit: 'coiled up', 'coiling like a snake') An Indian term for the primordial, dormant energy present in our body. It is supposed to reside in three-and-a-half coils at the base of the spine and can be awakened through meditation, yoga and other practices. A sudden awakening of the Kundalini can lead to a state of 'Kundalini Psychosis'.

Lao Tzu A famous Chinese philosopher who is believed to have lived in approximately the 4th century B.C. He is credited with writing the *Tao Te Ching*, one the most influential works of Taoism.

Meridians In Traditional Chinese Medicine, Qi is believed to flow through the body along clearly-defined and interconnected channels called 'meridians'. Disruptions to this Qi flow can manifest themselves as emotional or physical illness. The blockages or disruptions can be released using techniques such as acupuncture, massage, herbal medicine, meditation and mentally-directed sexual energy.

Microcosmic Orbit see **Small Orbit**

Neo-Tantric Western sexual practices based on a mix of Tantric, Taoist and various other philosophical and therapeutic lineages.

Qi (Chinese: 'Breath' or 'Air') The Life Force or Spiritual Energy that is inherent in all things.

Qi Gong (Chinese: 'Energy Cultivation') Chinese Inner Alchemy practices based on the movement of Qi through the body in specific patterns.

Sacred Sex An overall term for practices that use sexual activity for spiritual development.

Sexual Qi A particularly powerful form of Qi generated by sexual activity.

Shuang Xiu (Chinese: 'Dual Cultivation' or 'Paired Practices') See Dual Cultivation.

Small Orbit A Taoist internal alchemical practice of circulating Qi through the body using mental visualization.

Tai Chi or **Tai Chi Chuan** (Chinese: 'Supreme Ultimate Boxing') A Taoist system of physical movements originally designed for self-defence. Modern Tai Chi is used as a system of moving-meditation.

Tantra Indian sexual practices used for spiritual self-development.

Tantrika A skilled practitioner of Tantric practices.

Tan Tien A Chinese term for three major energy centres in the body. Most Taoist texts locate the Upper Tan Tien in the upper brain, the Middle Tan Tien in the heart and the Lower Tan Tien in the lower abdomen. The Lower Tan Tien is used extensively in Dual Cultivation, Inner Alchemy and the Martial Arts for storing Qi.

Tao (Chinese: 'The Way' or 'The Path') The Tao is the underlying and unchanging principle of the Universe and is a basic concept of Chinese philosophy. The Tao simply is.

Taoism An ancient Chinese philosophy. Taoism places emphasis upon spontaneity and teaches that everything in nature follows ways appropriate to itself. One of the fundamental tasks in life according to this philosophy is to discover our own way in harmony with nature or to 'become one with the Tao'.

Traditional Chinese Medicine (TCM) TCM is also known simply as Chinese or Oriental Medicine and refers to a wider range of practices developed over thousands of years including acupuncture, moxibustion and massage.

Yin and Yang The two fundamental, opposing but complementary, forces in the Universe. Yin (shady side of the mountain) is the passive, feminine aspect and Yang (sunny side of the mountain) is the active, masculine aspect.

Yoni The female sexual organs.

Acknowledgements

Writing a book is a challenge. Writing a book together, about a very intimate part of our lives, is a **big** challenge. The support and encouragement from our friends and family was the deciding factor that allowed us to overcome our natural resistance and concerns. We'd especially like to thank:

- Thierry for his encouragement to stick with the project even after our first frustratingly unsuccessful attempt to get something down on paper.
- Renild for the lovely drawings.
- Grietje who insisted that 'the woman's voice be heard'. Her hours of dialogue and subsequent editing with Mieke were the key to this crucial part of the story being told.
- Rebecca for pointing out that people can decide for themselves what to say!
- Linda for pointing out some potentially confusing British vs. American English expressions, and for reminding us that there are, indeed, nudist campsites in North America.
- The Finns for their clear, honest feedback.
- Our children for their patience and acceptance of their crazy parents.

Finally, we would like to acknowledge the work of the countless thousands of Taoist adepts who discovered and documented the techniques of Dual Cultivation. We are in your debt!

For a complete Findhorn Press catalogue, please contact:

Findhorn Press

305a The Park, Findhorn
Forres IV36 3TE
Scotland, UK
tel 01309 690582
fax 01309 690036
info@findhornpress.com
www.findhornpress.com